"Vanessa Farrell's well-written, captivating account of her personal journey in singleness is deeply inspiring. Each page bears powerful witness to God's providential care, and the points to ponder lead the reader on a trail toward greater hope, faith, and trust in His perfect timing."

Ann Marie Dewar, OBE, MA (Ed)
Educator, training designer/facilitator, and author

"Author Vanessa Farrell explores an issue facing a significant number of women. The revelation of her experiences is powerful, and her jewels on how to walk the path of waiting are transformative. It's a pleasure to read this body of work."

Lorna Fairweather, DHSc
Retired professor

"*Delayed Not Denied* is a book that hits the right chords and the right notes in the single life of a woman. As I read the book, I found that emotionally and spiritually it was very relatable: as Vanessa told her story, I saw myself. This book is a narrative of faith. It also tells us that there is hope in this walk with God, and we are not left out. Just as He was with Ruth and other great women of the Bible, God is very much the author of our life stories. You won't regret getting a copy for yourself. As a single woman, no matter your age, it will be one of the best investments you will ever make in your life as you journey with God."

Sonja Smith
Chief Librarian, Montserrat Public Library

"Vanessa Farrell has bared her soul in this book, vulnerably sharing her journey of singlehood in a world that often invalidates a single Christian woman's purpose. Part memoir, reflection, and research, this book shows readers that they are not alone in the quest to live a life that pleases God in every season of life."

Michelle Stimpson
Best-selling author, speaker, and journaling coach

"With remarkable vulnerability and personal stories that range from heartbreaking to hysterical, Vanessa Farrell shares her journey of singleness as she W.A.I.T.s for her future husband. Universal themes such as navigating blind dates, confronting infidelity, and battling menopause remind us of the many ties that bind us as women. The points to ponder at the end of each chapter invite readers to explore their own experiences. This book is a must-read for any woman who ever was, is, or will be single."

Sarah Strunk
Public health professional, marathon enthusiast

Delayed NOT DENIED

THE JOURNEY OF SINGLENESS
IT'S WORTH THE **W.A.I.T.**

VANESSA I. FARRELL

Delayed Not Denied:
The Journey of Singleness—It's Worth the W.A.I.T.
Author: **Vanessa I. Farrell**
Editor: **Linda Tate/Tate Communications**

Copyright©**2024** Vanessa Ingrid Health & Wellness Coaching, LLC. All rights reserved. No parts of this publication may be reproduced without written permission.

Vanessa Ingrid Health & Wellness Coaching, LLC.
PO Box 3275
Frederiksted, St. Croix
United States Virgin Islands (USVI)
www.vihealthcoaching.com
vfarrell@vihealthcoaching.com

Publisher: **Vanessa Ingrid Health & Wellness Coaching, LLC**

Scriptures are taken from the New International Version®, NIV® Copyright © 1973, 1978, 1984, 2011 by Biblica, Inc.® All rights reserved worldwide.

ISBN for Paperback: 979-8-9890507-5-8
ISBN for Hardback: 979-8-9890507-4-1
ISBN for E-Book: 979-8-9890507-3-4

Printed in the Unites States of America

Dedication

To God be all the glory!

To the amazing women in my family who supported me during the writing process: my mother, Mary, and my sisters, Patsy, Kim, Sandra, Jeanette, and Curleen; my niece Nicole; and my cousin Verna. I extend gratitude to my adopted mom, Carol, and my bonus sister, Tresa, who have both been a steady source of love and care.

To my dear friend Migdalia: I truly consider you the doula of this dream. I am grateful for your prayers, love, encouragement, and support over the last four years, ensuring that there was never a miscarriage of the assignment God placed in my heart. Thank you for sitting through hours of beachside reading, those soul-searching discussions, tears, and laughter as we worked through each breath and the pain of birthing this vision.

You have all, in your own special way, understood the W.A.I.T. and have unconditionally and without judgment loved me with such grace.

You are truly my circle; you are truly my tribe.
With love and deep appreciation.
Thank you!

Contents

Dedication vii
A Note to the Reader xi
Introduction xv

Chapter 1   My W.A.I.T. 1
Chapter 2   The Waiting Room 19
Chapter 3   Where It Began 25
Chapter 4   Love Awakened Before Its Time 33
Chapter 5   Education Was My Golden Ticket 43
Chapter 6   Sorry Can't Cool It! 55
Chapter 7   The Invisible Clock 65
Chapter 8   Juggling the Boys 73
Chapter 9   I Thought He Was the One 85
Chapter 10 Values and Boundaries 97
Chapter 11 What Do You Bring to the Table? 107
Chapter 12 Menopause Dared Me to Dump Dating 115

Epilogue 125
My Prayer 127
Resources for Further Exploration 129
About the Author 133

A Note to the Reader

Dear reader,

Thank you for reading *Delayed Not Denied: The Journey of Singleness—It's Worth the W.A.I.T.* I am delighted to have you on this journey with me.

Throughout this book, I share my personal journey through singleness to shedding light on common experiences that many women encounter on their own paths. Rather than a memoir solely focused on my own story, *Delayed Not Denied* is intended as an inspirational self-help book to guide you on your own journey. Consider it as a roadmap written by someone who has traveled the trail herself and can share some insight.

At the end of each chapter, you will find a section with points to ponder. This section offers you an opportunity for introspection and contemplation on the topic. Additionally, this book has an accompanying journal featuring thought-provoking prompts and questions designed to deepen your exploration of personal experiences, beliefs, and perspectives on the issues raised in each chapter. By journaling, you will uncover insights, attain clarity, and enhance your understanding of yourself as you navigate the realm of singleness. You can also explore these questions with a trusted friend, a church group, a book club, a coach, or a therapist. The possibilities are endless.

To gain various perspectives during the creation of this book, I conducted two surveys—one with single women over the age of thirty-five who desire marriage, the other with women who are currently or have been married. Throughout the book, you will come across select quotes from these surveys. May they serve as a reminder that you are not alone in your wait for the man God has specifically designed for you.

Once again, thank you for embarking on this journey with me. I hope that *Delayed Not Denied* inspires and encourages you as you navigate your path toward love and fulfillment.

In joyful expectation,
Vanessa

WHAT OTHER SINGLE WOMEN ARE SAYING

What is your definition of singleness?

- "Singleness to me is a period in life made for growth and preparation. Growth meaning working on oneself and being whole without another person's validation. Finding joy and what brings you joy. Preparation meaning making your body, soul, and mind right and ready to be a part of a healthy relationship."

- "This is a loaded question, as I recently saw a sermon by Pastor Michael Todd on singleness that shifted my perspective on this. Prior, I saw it as 'without commitment to another' (defined by another) but after, I see it as 'the opportunity to master oneself' (independent of another)."

—Single Woman Survey respondents

Introduction

"For I know the plans I have for you," declares the Lord, "plans to prosper you and not to harm you, plans to give you hope and a future."

JEREMIAH 29:11

As a woman over fifty who has never been married, I have my share of personal experiences and stories as I wait to be found by my future husband. I use the phrase "to be found" because of its biblical base: "He who finds a wife finds what is good and receives favor from the Lord" (Proverbs 11:22). I understand the mixed feelings and reactions that come with this delicate stage of life and the heavy cloak of uncertainty that can attempt to cover you and wear you down slowly. I understand the tears, and I know that hopelessness can be an enticing pillow to rest your head upon at night. But most important, I understand the vigilance it takes to guard your heart, mind, and soul during painful love and relationship experiences. The antidote to this dark space is constant prayer and a meaningful and deep relationship with God, trusting in His timing while fully loving and accepting the person looking back at you in the mirror.

Whether you are hoping for the fulfillment of a delayed promise or waiting for that day when your dreams and hopes come true and your heart smiles, remember, you are not alone. Like me, you might be waiting for a first or, perhaps, a second or third chance at love and marriage. Whatever the case, stay hopeful. I urge you to hang in there, be fearless, and not let your heart grow faint.

Despite a strong faith and the joys of living according to one's own whim, this journey of genuine singleness is often fraught with moments of loneliness, disappointments, heartaches, and hard lessons of life and love. Many of these I would prefer to skip over, forget, or downright deny. However, through these moments of loneliness, disappointments, heartaches, and lessons learned, I am discovering the actual value of my heart's desire and the significance of my W.A.I.T.

The notion of singleness, especially for women of a certain age, has many negative and positive connotations. Coupled with the word "loneliness," the very state of being single sets off many alarms in the court of public opinion. However, loneliness and singleness are two different concepts. I know from experience that being single can be fraught with moments of deep loneliness, but I also know that these bouts of loneliness are not the solid reason to escape my singleness. With maturity, I have learned that both concepts are two separate states that are not linked.

I define loneliness as "feeling alone (in this case, being single) and feeling bad about it." On the other hand, singleness is "not being married and not courting anyone with the expressed intention of getting married."

On this journey of singleness, it's easy to believe that the cause of our loneliness is being single and that the cure for loneliness is getting married. In a society where your singleness is questioned and not celebrated, this mindset is easily embraced. I, too, thought this to be true. Furthermore, I have come to learn from those who have journeyed similar paths that, as Alicia Britt Chole writes in *The Night Is Normal*, we must be careful "not to hope *in* relief, healing, restoration, or deliverance." "Our hope, biblically," Chole goes on to say, "is in a good and gracious God who is with us in every moment." As a woman of faith who is single yet desires to be married, my hope is grounded in God, who is merciful and ever present.

In seeking wisdom in this area, I have encountered several married women who have readily and adamantly declared that marriage is *not* the cure for loneliness! Interestingly, many women have confessed that being married has amplified or, in some cases, has shamefully exposed their true feelings of loneliness.

In one of my many conversations, I recall laughing deeply at the request to complete the lyrics to "If You Think You're Lonely Now," sung by Bobby Womack and later made popular by K-Ci & JoJo. I was left in deep reflection, as I had bellowed those lyrics many times without even understanding them and their underlying message.

In recent years and with continuous refinement, I have embraced the word "W.A.I.T." as an acronym for my personal touchstones. The concepts embodied in W.A.I.T. sum up how I genuinely feel about my journey of singleness. Arriving at this understanding was a process that took time, and it also took a lot of prayers and tears to understand, embrace, and wholeheartedly accept.

In the pages that follow, I will lay out what the W.A.I.T. means to me and how I have used it in life as I travel this journey of singleness. I share these touchstones not as a framework to be followed verbatim since we are all on our unique path but to let you know what has been working for me. That said, I hope that you will find some gems within my W.A.I.T. that you, too, can apply to your own life and journey of singleness.

As I **W.A.I.T.**, I have decided that I will continue to:

- Seek **WISDOM**. I will be open to gaining knowledge and understanding about myself, others, and the world around me.
- Keep **ASKING**. Knowing that the Bible says, "Ask, and it will be given to [me]," I will put my faith into action and remain patient.
- Be **INTENTIONAL**. I will embrace my singleness without shame and will be honest about my desire to marry.
- Trust God's **TIMING**. I know that His plans are greater than what I or society expect and that everything is divinely ordered.

THE JOURNEY OF SINGLENESS
W.A.I.T. TOUCHSTONES

W — Seek Wisdom
I will be open to gaining knowledge and understanding about myself, others and the world around me.

The tree of life symbolizes the growth and expansion of knowledge by seeking wisdom. You do so by branching out and exploring different areas and sources of information.

A — Keep Asking
Knowing that the Bible says, "Ask, and it will be given to [me]," I will put my faith in action and remain patient.

The praying hand symbolizes the act of asking and seeking guidance from God. You do so by humbly approaching the throne of grace and earnestly requesting what you want.

I — Be Intentional
I will embrace my singleness without shame and will be honest about my desire to marry.

The heart and key symbolizes the act of unlocking and revealing your true intentions. You do so by being open and honest about your heart's desires for love and what you want in a husband and in a relationship.

T — Trust God's Timing
I know that His plans are greater than what I or society expect and that everything is divinely ordered.

The butterfly emerging from its chrysalis symbolizes transformation and growth. Only God knows the exact timing of events in your life. You do so by being patient while cultivating who you are as you get ready for the husband God has for you.

created by Vanessa I. Farrell

These internal touchstones are anchors that keep me grounded when my total being becomes overwhelmed without warning at the slightest trigger that reminds me of my singleness. They steady me whenever I erupt into sudden bouts of weeping, whining, and personal protesting, or even when I go so far as to question God's timing: "When, Lord, when?" They are my mental map to navigate to my sanity.

As I have walked and worked through these touchstones in my daily life, the decision to be obedient and to surrender my journey fully to God has not always been an enticing option or even the choice that I selected. Still, with age and experience, I have found that my path has become clearer.

I wrote this book not just to document my experience as a single woman with a strong desire to marry but also to let other single women realize they are not alone. This book is my way of looking you square in the eye and saying, "Sis, I see you, and I understand; yes, I truly do!" I hope to encourage you and to reveal how you can tilt toward the bright and better side in making the most out of your W.A.I.T.

I hope the story of my experiences on this journey of singleness and waiting inspires you. May we never forget to give glory to God for keeping us in a place of contentment and joyful expectation. Most important, I hope it reminds you that your heart's desire for love is simply delayed and not denied.

Points to Ponder

- Being single can be a challenging and sometimes discouraging period in life, especially when you desire to be married. Take a moment to think about your own journey of singleness and ways you are intentionally nurturing your mind, body, and soul during this time.

- Remember that love has its own timing. Despite the long wait, trust that the right person is being prepared for you. Have faith that at the right time your paths will cross and that you will meet the person who is meant to be by your side.

WHAT OTHER SINGLE WOMEN ARE SAYING

Why am I not married?

- "It is just a part of life. I made bad choices in some instances, and other times, I refused to settle for less than I deserved."

- "I have had bad experiences in past relationships."

- "Timing is also a factor. Great person, wrong timing."

- "I have not met the right person, and I enjoy being single. Maybe too much. LOL."

- "Men do not stay with me because I refuse to be in a sexual relationship; everyone left. They are not living according to the Word. Some men were clergy, which means nothing to me."

—*Single Woman Survey respondents*

Chapter One
MY W.A.I.T.

Wait for the Lord; be strong and take heart and wait for the Lord.
PSALMS 27:14

Being single and over fifty years old is sometimes a tough pill to swallow, especially when your heart desires marriage. As the Good Book says, "Hope deferred makes the heart sick, but a desire fulfilled is a tree of life" (Proverbs 13:12). As I read this verse, I ask myself, "What's the state of my heart when it's teetering on the reality of delay and the hope that my heart's desire to be married will not be denied?" But until my hopes are realized, what are the rules of engagement? How do I date while I wait? And most important, how do I wait well? These are some of the courageous conversations I find myself engaged in today; they are also questions I wish I had discussed with my younger self.

As I share my journey as a single woman with you, I will consider my dating, love, life experiences, and lessons through my W.A.I.T. touchstones. My story is not intended to bash or scorn men nor to seek sympathy or supporters. Instead, I intend to share the truth of my journey while using my experiences—whether daring, devastating, or delightful—as love's life lessons. I hope that my experience will be a source of encouragement or wisdom for you on your journey of singleness.

In the next few pages, I will explain how I use these W.A.I.T. touchstones to tap into my faith to sustain me and draw strength, hope, and joy along my journey.

TOUCHSTONE #1

> Wisdom is supreme; therefore get wisdom. Though
> it cost all you have, get understanding.
>
> PROVERBS 4:7

Seek Wisdom
I will be open to gaining knowledge and understanding about myself, others and the world around me.

The tree of life symbolizes the growth and expansion of knowledge by seeking wisdom. You do so by branching out and exploring different areas and sources of information.

I am curious by nature. My mother would say I am "too nosy," and my friends think I am inquisitive. The men I have dated have also often said that I am full of questions. However, I think this question of asking questions is all about perspective. Growing up, I would meet a person for the first time, and through casual and easy conversations, I would learn about their life story by the end of the encounter. The pace at which I connected with and learned about someone so well after such a short chance meeting would baffle friends and family.

As I entered adulthood, I still embodied this curiosity, but my dating experiences began teaching me that most men were not always fond of my data-gathering desires. Some pacified me with lies and half-truths. Others looked at me sideways, trying to make sense of my inquiry, while others blatantly ignored me.

Eventually, I just stopped: I stopped asking the "right" questions, I stopped asking the "deep" questions, and to my fault, I stopped asking the "Are you just wasting my time?" questions. To gain the favor and acceptance of my love interests, I found myself sacrificing my God-given nature and innate characteristic of seeking knowledge.

This shift toward an "ask-no-hard-questions" approach was unnatural to me, and as a result, my dating life suffered tremendously. This approach left me perpetually unsatisfied and upset, and I found myself living in my head. I would create stories and positively amplify the character traits of my dates and my dating situation; the stories I imagined were as far from the truth as east is from west. Sometimes, I would think I was involved in a meaningful adult relationship when, in the mind of my love interest, we were just going with the flow, kicking it, or even worse, just being friends. I would be left puzzled, deciphering the reality of my situation, "…say what?" voicing my shock of my discovery.

One too many of these scenarios proved that this was a flawed approach to dating. This approach of repressing my desire to ask questions of the men I dated, coupled with the imaginary stories I created about these men, hindered the establishment of a meaningful long-term relationship, let alone marriage. I needed to seek wisdom on healthy, intentional dating and love and what life was like in the context of marriage. I had to go back to the basics by seeking wisdom and guidance from other women who had gone down the path of marriage or have been in long-term relationships. I asked them what it is like to be married, what it is like to be in a long-term relationship, what has worked for them and what has not worked. I was curious, so I asked about the red flags that we as women see but choose to ignore and what those nonnegotiables are. I specifically asked the married women if they would do life again with the same person and why. The answer to the latter question was always met with hesitation and hovered closer to "no" on the marriage spectrum. But through deeper conversation, it becomes clear that, in retrospect, many of these women wished they had had more insight, had asked the right questions, and had had a better understanding of what they were signing up for relative to marriage.

I recall having a conversation with a dear friend who was married. She said, "Vanessa, marriage is like flies in a glass jar: those who are inside want to get out, and those who are outside want to get in. So don't rush. *Wait* for love to find you. It will happen." I had just turned thirty, and her words were powerful and have stuck with me. I easily understood these words of wisdom with their gems of patience, order, and timing. Over the years, I continued to seek out these cherished encounters; I kept these gems in my heart and mind and journaled furiously on them.

I am continually steeped in conversations and books about dating, love, relationships, and marriage. I have listened to hundreds of podcasts, YouTube videos, and TED Talks, and I have continued to interview women informally on the topic. I have bought into membership programs, workshops, and seminars on love and relationships. I am so invested in what others say on the topic that I sent out a survey while writing this book to gather insights and thoughts from other women who were thirty-five years and older—unmarried with the desire to be married. It was surprising to see that 121 women responded to the questionnaire; their responses are shared throughout this book in the sections titled "What other single women are saying."

We may think that it is only human to find our own path and that we should learn from personal experiences. Although this is true to an extent, I look at life differently. I believe that in addition to our own experiences, we can also learn and gain wisdom from other people's experiences. I look at their life journeys, and if there are things I could learn that would prevent me from going down a difficult path or, better yet, make my life easier or more enjoyable, how could that in any way be a bad thing?

What I discovered in my quest for enlightenment is that when it comes to love, it doesn't matter your race, religious belief, gender, or age—we all have an innate desire to be loved and be in love. However, we all want to be wise about love and our choices to get and keep the love our heart so deeply desires.

When I was younger, people often told me that I was wise beyond my years. Despite the fact that I was single, my friends have always come to me for relationship advice. They sometimes say, "Girl, you know so much! Why aren't you married or in a relationship?" That question has frequently made me unhappy, and I have wondered the same thing, too. However, over the years, I have learned to remind myself and my friends that it's just not the right time for me yet. Here is what I know for sure about wisdom:

- Wisdom is God talking: listen!
- Wisdom can saves lives.
- Wisdom eases the stresses of daily living.
- Wisdom saves you from heartaches and heartbreaks.
- Wisdom shows you your value and solidifies your sense of self-worth.
- Wisdom gives you the strength to set and keep boundaries.
- Wisdom is a secret shortcut to happiness and joy.
- Wisdom is a gift that keeps on giving.
- Wisdom is the friend you did not listen to but is still there for you when all hell breaks loose.

I will continue to seek wisdom, as it brings clarity to my life and gives a better understanding of who I am at this moment.

TOUCHSTONE #2

> Ask, and it will be given to you; seek, and you will find;
> knock, and the door will be opened to you.
>
> MATTHEW 7:7

A

Keep Asking
Knowing that the Bible says, "Ask, and it will be given to [me]," I will put my faith in action and remain patient.

The praying hand symbolizes the act of asking and seeking guidance from God. You do so by humbly approaching the throne of grace and earnestly requesting what you want.

As a believer, I find that many verses in the Bible encourage me to ask God for whatever I need whenever I need it. Without reservation, I have often cited verses about asking, such as Matthew 7:7, which says, "Ask, and it will be given to you." Also, there is John 14:1, which tells me, "You may ask for anything in my name, and I will do it." And two chapters later, in John 16:24, is a further affirmation: "…Ask and you will receive, and your joy will be complete." Then, one day I unexpectedly came across Matthew 6:8, which says, "…for your Father knows what you need before you ask him." And with that, I was stumped.

As a baby Christian, I was confused about when and how I should ask God for what I needed—especially when it pertained to my relationship with men. When it came to dating, I was terrified that asking a man for what I wanted outright from a relationship would somehow "rock the boat" and strain the friendship with my love interest. Furthermore, I did not ask because it might doom the chance of moving the friendship to the stage of a committed relationship. As a result, I dwelled in a space of fear that only left me in a world of false assumptions and living in my head about the person I was dating. Over time, I realized that most of my assumptions were absolutely false.

I didn't know I could ask God about these things. As a young woman in my early years of dating, I never thought of just sitting with God and having real talk. When I say, "real talk," I mean that heart-to-heart talk about my fears, my vulnerabilities, my pain, my anger, my loneliness, and my heart's desires when it comes to men and truths about dating. I thought that was an area of my life I need not bother Him with. This dynamic of trying to do it on my own and not asking God for what's best for me was exacerbated when I found myself in sexual relationships. I was definitely not going to ask Him for anything at that point. After all, I had broken the cardinal rule—and my feelings of brokenness and shame were the consequences of my transgressions.

As I mature in life and the arena of dating, I have no fear of "asking" because He wants me to ask. The verse that perplexed me decades ago takes on a whole new meaning because I understand that He knows what's best for me. Today, I am older and wiser, and I have no fear of asking God for everything or talking to Him about anything. He's not a genie that grants me all my wishes. in fact, He's quite the opposite! The times He has said no in my life have significantly outweighed those times when He has said yes. There's nothing I do these days without checking in with God. And even more important, I don't shy away from having courageous conversations with any man I date.

I have learned that dating is not for mating but for data gathering, and although some men are honest in sharing, most are not, especially in the early stages of dating. However, whenever I have not asked the right questions, I have not gotten the right answers, and this has left me operating on faulty data. The revelation of deception has on some occasions created a deep sense of betrayal, leaving me questioning everything and everyone in the world around me—especially the value of love and relationships.

Despite these betrayals, I look for the lessons and ask myself, "How did I contribute to these experiences?" I would be the first to say that I have knowingly ignored red flags, white lies, and subtle indiscretions. At the same time, I, too, have been guilty of creating beautiful stories in my head about my dates. I always choose to see the best in people, but in my dating experiences, I have sometimes been delusional. On the other hand, maybe, just maybe, I have been told the truth, but I have heard only what I wanted to hear and my interpretation was off. Essentially, I prevented myself from gaining clarity to fuzzy answers or trusting my intuition. Most important, I know that sex makes for murky memories—so at all costs, don't mix data gathering with sex.

I recall viewing an episode of the reality TV show "The Millionaire Matchmaker," and hearing host Patti Stanger say "dating is not for mating, but data gathering." This quote has stuck with me over the years as it reflects the belief that dating should be approached with a strategic mindset, gathering information, and assessing compatibility rather than solely focusing on finding a lifelong partner. Basically, it's vital to get to know the people you are dating and quickly move on if it's very clear they are not whom or what you desire in life or in love.

So today, I can't say that I always get it right or that I have gotten what I have asked God for in terms of a mate. Still, I am committed to continually asking, listening, and learning, but most important, seeking His knowledge and wisdom and a spirit of discernment.

TOUCHSTONE #3

> Delight yourself in the Lord, and he will give you the desires of your heart.
> PSALMS 37:4

Be Intentional
I will embrace my singleness without shame and will be honest about my desire to marry.

The heart and key symbolizes the act of unlocking and revealing your true intentions. You do so by being open and honest about your heart's desires for love and what you want in a husband and in a relationship.

Without an iota of doubt, I believe that human beings are innately wired to love and be loved. It is not a *want* or some frivolous desire that just pulls on our heartstrings. Instead, love is a *need*—a need so profound that we would go to the ends of the earth to pursue it and claim it; we would even die for it. Despite this fact, deep and heavy emotions restrain us as women, denying us the ability to publicly announce our heart's longing for real love and marriage.

I understand the position that so many women have taken when it comes to being in a relationship with men because I was one of those women who shouted from the mountaintop and joined in the single ladies' anthem to declare "I don't need a man." This narrative of self-sufficiency and guarding our hearts when it comes to men is so ingrained in our minds that a shift would be a monumental task that many women do not have the mental capacity or willpower to do. This narrative of self-protection at all costs has roots that are deep, dark, and widely distributed, deriving from multiple sources of infractions.

Back then, we did not have a word to describe it, but today, we know it to be trauma, that is, a deeply distressing or disturbing experience. Like so many other women, we may find ourselves on the receiving end of abuse and mistreatment by the men we have entrusted our hearts to or whom we have pledged before God and society to love 'til death do us part.

In dating, I have had some beautiful encounters, but I've also had my share of setups, setbacks, and life-altering experiences—some of which I will share later in this book. There were the broken promises, lies, and indiscretions. There was the perpetual cheating that created another human being. There was the talk of marriage and a future together only to renege without explanation. There were controlling tendencies, narcissism, and fearmongering. And let's not forget the announcement of a wedding to someone else the following month while the man was in hot pursuit of my love and attention.

These incidents only hardened my heart and made me want to draw the line on love, join the nunnery, and take the pledge of chastity. But deep down in my heart, I knew there was a place for love, a place that was beautiful, a place where there was joy, a place of peace as God so rightly intended it, and my soul yearned for that. I felt in my heart that if love, so beautiful, coupled with joy and peace, was what my heart desired, then what were the pieces that knitted them together? And what made this love so elusive? Most important, what made my soul yearn for love when the past was peppered with pains that pierced my soul so powerfully? These questions seemed so simple, yet they were complicated and puzzling.

I started with what I knew and what came easily for me: praying and journaling. I began praying intensely and added Priscilla Shirer's book *Fervent: A Woman's Battle Plan to Serious,*

Specific and Strategic Prayer to my morning devotional time. I consistently journaled after each chapter about what I had learned and about how I honestly felt and what I wanted in love. I had to be intentional and honest with myself and get clear about my values, my needs, and my desires in future relationships. I learned that I had to prioritize myself and do what was best for my sanity and me.

I also saw areas in my life that needed tending to, like nurturing my self-confidence as well as creating and maintaining boundaries. In doing so, I quickly realized that perhaps I needed to take a break from dating or, at best, be more intentional about the men I dated—knowing that even though men may approach me and pick me, I needed to get better at choosing them.

This was an intentional journey that made me do the following:

- Take the time to reflect on my past relationships to better understand what worked and what didn't and to spot some of the patterns I have that could have contributed to the demise of the relationship.
- Recognize what my values are and what is important to me in a relationship. I am clear that for me to thrive in a relationship, I need honesty, trust, communication, and respect.
- Acknowledge how important boundaries are and how maintaining them is so pivotal. I am very clear about what I will not tolerate, and I don't have any qualms about communicating my boundaries. This position, however, takes the most practice and hypervigilance.
- Learn that people are not mind readers and that sharing expectations early makes it easier to communicate and leaves less room for misinterpretation. This could be as simple as

saying "I would prefer if you called me versus texting" or as difficult as stating "I don't want to have children or mind someone else's child."
- Refrain from rushing into any relationship, no matter how handsome or fine the man is or how fast you think time is flying by. Taking the time to get to know a person gives a better perspective of their values and life goals.

I vow to be intentional about what I want in love; I feel this is the path to a fulfilling and healthy relationship. I cannot be secretly asking God for my heart's desire while my public actions are misaligned and lack intention.

TOUCHSTONE #4

> There is a time for everything, and a season for
> every activity under the heavens....
> ECCLESIASTES 3:1

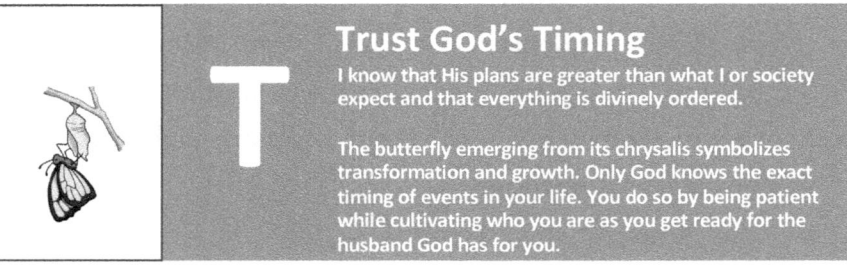

Trust God's Timing
I know that His plans are greater than what I or society expect and that everything is divinely ordered.

The butterfly emerging from its chrysalis symbolizes transformation and growth. Only God knows the exact timing of events in your life. You do so by being patient while cultivating who you are as you get ready for the husband God has for you.

In a world measured in seasons and phases, humans are indeed time beings. We consistently tap our phones to see the time, we take incessant glimpses of the watches on our wrists, we stare at clocks on our walls, and we circle dates on the calendar so we can keep track of progress and changes. The consciousness of time is subtly clouded in our minds and entrenched in our systems.

Our lives, too, have been chunked off in time segments, leading us to believe that there is a mandated time frame when certain life events should happen—like marriage! When people used to ask me why I was still single, part of me literally died. You may say, "Vanessa, that sounds a bit harsh," and it does. But it wasn't me who was dying as a person; it was my desire and the hope of my intention that was being chipped away each time the question came up. As I got older, I dreaded those moments. I became defensive and felt a bit of hopelessness because it was the one area in my life that I felt I had little or no control over.

It was hard enough when questions of my singleness came up in general conversations with friends, family, and acquaintances. But when that question was posed in tandem with my lack of children, especially when that question was asked on dates, I wanted to just jump on the table and scream, "I don't know!" This line of questioning was often emotionally depleting.

Truth be told, it was exasperating! My answers never seemed to satisfy the listener; they seemed to be eagerly waiting for me to spill some juicy, jolting justification for my singleness. I had no such explanation, and if I'd had the inkling of one (we all do), I just wasn't going to share.

Then without warning, the craziest thing started happening, I, too, began questioning myself. There I was, asking myself, "Vanessa, why are you still single?"

The frustration was real, and I began feeling that my thoughts were too scattered and that I needed time to rein them in. So, in true Vanessa form, I carved out time to pray, reflect, and journal on two questions: "What am I looking for in a mate?" and "Why do I think I'm still single?" I can't say that I emerged with perfect clarity to address these questions or that I felt more equipped to answer the piercing inquiries of other people about my singleness. But over time, I felt more grounded in the certainty that I was on my own divinely planned path and that it was all about timing.

I am less frazzled when people ask me these questions today, and although I do not have a canned answer that I recite to inquiring minds, I know without a doubt that I am truthful and clear. What works well for me is that I evaluate the situation, try to understand the intention of the person who is asking the question, and answer accordingly. This does not mean that there is a lack of consistency or that I am wishy-washy, but it does mean that I am much better at being clear and more discerning than I have been in the past. So, depending on the situation I am confronted with, I would answer in one of the following ways:

- "I'm very happy with my life as it is right now." This indicates that I am content with my current situation and don't feel the need to be married to be happy or to be a whole person. (This is for the person who seems very perplexed that I can possibly be happy without a man or not married at this age.)
- "I'm still waiting for the right person." This signals that I am actively seeking a partner and that I am open to the possibility of marriage. (This is appropriate if I am on a date with someone, I find interesting or in conversation with a person, male or female, who genuinely cares about me and might be curious about how things are going in the dating, love, and marriage department of my life.)
- "Marriage isn't the only measure of a fulfilling life." This notes the fact that there are many ways to find happiness and fulfillment in life and that being married is just one of them. (This is usually for the folks who have been married since they were nineteen and who now, at sixty-nine, just cannot understand why, at my age, I am still single. They seem genuinely sorry for me. This is exacerbated if it appears to them that I am living my best life without being coupled up. The unspoken question becomes "how dare you?" They are never forthcoming in these conversations, but sometimes I feel the insinuation that not having children is a selfish mindset.)
- "I prefer to keep my personal life private." This makes clear that I am not comfortable discussing my personal life

with this person under any circumstance. (This is for those random questions you get from folks who are seemingly judgmental, those times when you intuitively have a feeling of being taunted. You are not being sensitive—it is just a feeling that no one can explain but you.)

It has taken some time, but today I feel assured that things will fall into place in the exact way God intended. I commit to staying open to the possibilities of love, and I have embraced the fact that meeting the right mate and getting married is not in my time, not in society's time, but all in God's time.

Points to Ponder

- Creating personal guiding principles or touchstones can provide a solid foundation for navigating your single journey. These principles serve as truths that keep you grounded and encouraged, especially during moments of loneliness, solitude, or sadness.
- Remember that personal principles can vary from person to person and may evolve over time. The ultimate goal is to establish a solid foundation upon which you can confidently embrace and navigate your singleness.

WHAT OTHER SINGLE WOMEN ARE SAYING

How do you stay encouraged/hopeful during this time of waiting?

- "Enjoy my life. Explore new activities. Focus on work. Date quality men. Keep up a body care, self-care, and beauty regimen that makes me feel sexy. Wear undergarments and clothing that make me feel attractive."

- "I just continue with my day to day and say it's going to happen soon."

- "Remembering God's promise of giving me my heart's desires and knowing nothing happens before its time. God's timing and promises are greater than anything we could ever imagine. By focusing my attention on my relationship with Him, it keeps me grounded."

—Single Woman Survey respondents

Chapter Two
THE WAITING ROOM

> An excellent wife who can find? She is far more precious than jewels. The heart of her husband trusts in her, and he will have no lack of gain. She does him good, and not harm, all the days of her life.
>
> —PROVERBS 31:10-12

Do I think I am in the "waiting room" of my life? Do I believe that I am just sitting and waiting to be found? Do I envision my future husband magically opening my waiting room door and calling my name? Do I then look up with butterflies, a flutter, and eyes as bright as a diamond, ready to be swept off my feet into the land of happily ever after? Do I think that the waiting room exists? Is it pleasant or challenging to wait, and most important, how do I behave while in the waiting room when my wait lingers beyond the limits of my patience?

Within the waiting room, I encounter other single women. Like me, some have never been married, others have had failed engagements, and still others have had long-term love relationships. I have also met women who are divorced and those who are widowed, and occasionally, some married women grace us with their presence in the waiting room. The thought of being married and residing in the waiting room may seem unsettling to many. Still, to understand this concept, we need to realize that despite being married, many women are still in the waiting room, patiently waiting for the man they married to evolve into the man of their dreams or, more to the point, the man God intended him to be. Many such women have confided in me that they regrettably married the promise of their partner's potential rather than the person who stood before them on their wedding day—hence they wait.

Regardless of the reason a woman has taken a seat in the waiting room, there is one thing that we all have in common: we are waiting, and despite the unknown, we just have to W.A.I.T. As we wait, there is no better way to perfectly sum up this experience than to view it as being similar to sitting in the waiting room of a doctor's office, waiting for your turn to receive medical attention. In this case, a few things are certain: we know (and have faith) that our turn will come, and we know our name will be called. However, the part that makes us most anxious and, at times, hopeless is that we just don't know when we'll be called. Our behavior in the waiting room can range from scanning the waiting room and curiously wondering about the stories and maladies of others and what brought them here. We glance at the clock repeatedly, hoping that time will move faster. We fidget in our seats, tap our feet, scroll on our phones, or flip through outdated magazines to distract ourselves from the mounting impatience. The minutes tick by slowly, and we can't help but feel a sense of restlessness. The atmosphere is charged with a mix of nervous energy and anticipation. Finally, a wave of relief washes over you when your name is called.

Well, my waiting room is a metaphorical but powerful place that exists in both my heart and my mind. The heart embodies my desire, my longing, and my excitement and expectation of love. The mind, on the other hand, is more practical and contemplates things like the values my partner should have and the criteria he should meet. The mind is also sinister, and in many instances, I would be left to grapple with feelings of fear, doubt, and insecurities related to being single and wating for romantic love.

While there are no physical walls, windows, doors, or ceiling in my waiting room, emerging from my waiting room to what society coins as "happily ever after" seems somewhat elusive. This is not only evident to me who is waiting but also to the spectators of my life.

I will be the first to say that waiting is one of the hardest parts of the human condition. The word "waiting" itself commands stillness, yet taken another way, it is a verb that requires action and lots of faith. For me, taking action are those times of deep self-reflection and getting to know who I am, what my needs are, and what I seek in a mate. Action is engaging in and learning new skills as well as pursuing my goals and dreams. Most important, action is strengthening my faith by cultivating a deeper relationship with God.

I know for sure that my waiting room experience has defined and continues to define who I truly am to the core. Over the years, I have seen myself at my best and my worst. My waiting room has exposed my weaknesses, and it has built my courage beyond what I thought I was capable of. In my waiting room, I have experienced instances when I felt victimized and other times when I felt victorious and unshakable. In my waiting room, I have often found myself in a state of anticipation and uncertainty. At times, my emotions have been raw and frayed, with a blend of hope, worry, and impatience. In these moments, time has seemed to stretch beyond my waiting capacity, and every passing minute has felt like an eternity.

Despite these sobering realities, I have learned that my waiting room is not a place to fret or grow faint; I have learned that the choices I make during this time are all mine, and so are the consequences. I can withdraw and hang drapes of isolation that allow my waiting room to become a dark dungeon of torture and oppression that makes me weak and vulnerable, or I can be the woman who draws the drapes and opens the blinds to reveal my strength, showing the waiting room as a process of change that furnishes and conditions me for a more productive and joyful life.

This realization did not occur supernaturally or overnight. It took a major shift in my mindset, but I have embraced my waiting room as a place of transformation, reinvention, and renewal. Similar to the well-timed life cycle of the beloved butterfly, I see myself emerging from the waiting room as a beautiful, bold champion, an unstoppable woman launched into the love story she longs for in God's divine timing.

Points to Ponder

- Do you consider yourself in a waiting room? In today's fast-paced world, waiting can be challenging and burdensome, particularly when it comes to matters of the heart. How are you truly feeling during this season of waiting?

- Remember that love can find you at any time and at any age. Continue to embrace your journey, cultivate meaningful relationships, and live a fulfilling life.

WHAT OTHER SINGLE WOMEN ARE SAYING

What have the females in your life told you about men and being in relationships?

- "Often that you're better off not being married. Marriage is hard, and you give up some of yourself to make the other person happy."

- "Never trust a man. All men cheat. Men have no feelings. Men should take care of you."

- "The ones who are married wish they were single again, and the single ones are like me, wishing they were married. I've been told that I have to accept some level of baggage in older men 'cause they all have it. It's just about what you are willing to accept."

—Single Woman Survey respondents

Chapter Three
WHERE IT BEGAN

Let the heavens rejoice, let the earth be glad; let the sea resound, and all that is in it. Let the fields be jubilant, and everything in them.

PSALMS 96:11

I was a 1970 baby, born on Montserrat, a tiny island of thirty-nine-and-a-half square miles in the Caribbean Sea. I grew up in Parsons, a small, quiet village made up of thirty-seven government-built scheme houses nestled in the foothills of Chances Peak Mountain. The beauty of my home island will be forever imprinted on my heart and in my mind.

Montserrat is affectionately called "The Emerald Isle of the Caribbean" for its lush green mountains and breathtaking landscape that blends harmoniously with the sparkling blue Caribbean Sea. Montserrat's nickname also bears roots in both its rich Irish ancestry and its resemblance to the lushness of coastal Ireland.

Remembering my childhood and youth on Montserrat brings with it a wealth of nostalgia. I can still envision the sun's golden rays dancing as if to the rhythms of calypso music on the surface of the sea during the day, only to be eclipsed by the awaiting horizon at dusk. Evenings brought a gentle breeze that not only cooled the hot Caribbean air but also beckoned Montserrat's people to slow down, to rest, and to connect.

What I miss most about growing up on this gem of an island is the abundance of fresh fruits she bore. I can still smell the sweet fragrance of those juicy mangoes, pineapples, soursops, and bananas about to be devoured and still see the tempting sight of ripening fruits like papaya, genips, and tamarind, oh so colorfully towering on trees just beyond my reach.

We were blessed to be home to the Montserrat Soufrière Hills waterfall, located near the Soufrière Hills volcano in the southern part of the island. The falls provided a peaceful setting amid wildlife and lush flora, and unbeknownst to us, a volcano that kept deep, dark secrets lying dormant below. I enjoyed watching the spectacular exhibition of rushing water cascading down the falls on stair-like rocks into a nature-made pool offering an area for swimming and relaxation.

When I was growing up, the population of Montserrat hovered around eight thousand and was twelve thousand at its peak. Living on an island that size was comforting, as faces always looked familiar and a family member was never far away. Except for a three-year stint that took me to the neighboring island of St. Kitts from the ages of ten to thirteen, I completed most of my primary and secondary school education on Montserrat.

Years later in 1995, almost a decade after immigrating to the United States, my beloved Montserrat was ravished by the deadly eruption of the Soufrière Hill volcano. The eruption was powerful: it reconfigured the shape of the island, took lives and livelihoods, and displaced a majority of the island's residents. The population living on the island was reduced to just under five thousand people—where it stands today.

I share the details of my roots as a way to give insight and context to my story and to immortalize the many once-beautiful settings on the island of Montserrat that have been ravished by the volcano and that no longer exist.

MY JOURNEY

Like me, many women my age in the Parsons community were raised in single-parent households, often headed by a female or single mother. This family makeup was a common thing; it was mostly what we saw and became accustomed to. On our street, one family had a mother and a father in the home.

The hustle of women still looking tired from the previous day's grind, rising at the crack of dawn and readying themselves and their children for the day ahead was the standard of our society. With a well-orchestrated performance from devotions at dawn to dinner at dusk and everything in between, these women ran a tight ship, and they did not complain—at least, my mother did not. No one was there to take the boys and teach them to be men of stellar character or to alleviate the pressure of mothers. The idea of easing the stress mothers felt to give them a break from the children for a day or two so they could have some "me time" or to indulge in a bit of self-care was a foreign concept.

I watched my mother, a single mother of six, toil from sunup to sundown to make ends meet for the family. She supplemented her income as a housekeeper with various odd jobs that she did before and after work and on weekends. She planted a garden that produced lots of fruits and vegetables, which she shared with neighbors, and she still managed to bake batches of bread, cakes, and other delicacies for her family and any who stopped by.

My mother and the other amazing women in my neighborhood held down the fort and quietly did what they had to do to raise their children. In my eyes, though I was not able to verbalize it at the time, they were truly the epitome of strong Black women. As I was growing up, my young mind unconsciously recorded the reality of my upbringing as a way of life. I am certainly guilty of taking it a step further by embellishing and idolizing the role and vision of the strong Black woman.

I emerged into my young adult years with the unbalanced imprint of a woman's roles in the household and the world. This was coupled with a limited understanding of the dynamics of the mother/father or husband/wife relationship. This is in no way a criticism of my upbringing, but that was the reality of how things were at that time, and that reality couldn't be undone.

With maturity comes understanding, especially as it pertains to matters of heart, life, love, and living. With this clarity, I will be the first to say that the strong Black women who raised me were literally forced to be strong. They did not voluntarily take on this role. From the countless conversations I have had with these women, including my mother, grandmother, godmother, aunties, and girlfriends, I have learned that many of them were dealt a bad hand. In their quest for love, committed relationships, and marriage, they were faced with rejection and, in some cases, isolation with a few children in tow whom they had to raise alone.

From the remnants of their pain and trauma, these so-called strong Black women drew their source of strength and survival. They never signed up to be the strong Black women that society labeled them. Still for some reason, they found it difficult, even too painful, to shy away from these labels and stereotypes, so they just reluctantly rolled with the situations they found themselves in.

The realities of my upbringing by a single unwed mother of six and an absentee father can unleash all kinds of judgment in the court of public opinion. For starters, some may observe the fact that I am not married and say that I am a product of my environment. However, I would be the first to challenge that thought by saying, "Oh, no, I am not." This knee-jerk response is not to look down on my humble beginnings or in any way publicly declare that I have arrived but instead to say that there are aspects of my upbringing that I have embraced and others that I have allowed to die on the vine or that I have downright rejected. I can further challenge that thought as I look at my siblings with whom I grew up—and if I had to calculate their combined years of marriage to their spouses, it would be almost sixty years. This is an important fact as it shows different paths, journeys and outcomes despite the same environment in which we were nurtured.

I was never taught to make marriage a part of my life plan, and it was never discussed in my home or among my circle of friends. Whenever there was a conversation about marriage, it was either looked upon as a fairy tale or something that happened to other people. To be honest, marriage was rarely discussed, and I did not see it as being a good or bad thing—it just was something I was indifferent about.

As a young woman growing up, I did not have marriage as an aspiration drummed into my head. Instead, I was consistently told by the adult women in my life: "You need to go to school, get a good education, graduate high school (with no babies), and go on to college. Once you finish college, get a good job and make your own money. You should never—ever depend on a man to take care of you or buy you stuff. Get your own everything, including a house and car. Always have your own (money); do not depend on a man for anything." And if that weren't clear enough, the conversation was topped off with "You can do bad all by yourself."

With all my heart, I know that this advice came from a place of love and wanting the best for me as I ventured into navigating life and womanhood independently. The women in my life wanted to protect me; they wanted to save me from the heartache of financial hardship, disappointment, and the betrayal of men, and most important, they wanted a better life (than they had had) for me. These narratives were, in the minds of these women, a surefire recipe for protection and triumph, a protective factor from the life they endured as women who had been left to navigate the daily demands of raising children and running a household alone. Many of these women placed their desire for love, relationship, or even marriage on hold; some placed it on the back burner, and even more heart-wrenching, many of these women put love "on the shelf" to raise their children.

As children grow up and become independent, their mothers have an undeniable and heartwarming sense of pride and joy in raising responsible young people to send out into the world. I can recall the joy in my mother's eyes and the eyes of so many other women in my life when I accomplished educational milestones and advanced to the other mile markers in my life. I believe that behind my mother's beaming heart was probably a record playing in her mind that went something like this: "I don't know how I made it raising these six children alone, but I am grateful to see the fruits of my labor, love, and sacrifice, and I give all the praise to God." I can only imagine that she felt my success was truly her success—and I believe it is.

Points to Ponder

- Memories of your upbringing can have a major influence on your relationship with men. Thinking about these memories can be a powerful way to gain insight into your current mindset and behaviors.

- Remember that you are not responsible for the circumstances of your childhood or the experiences you may have had. However, it is important to seek the help and support you need to heal from any childhood hurts or traumas that may be impacting your current relationships. Consider seeking therapy, counseling, or other forms of support to address and heal from any unresolved issues. By doing this inner work, you can create a solid foundation for future love relationships and approach them with wholeness and healing.

WHAT OTHER SINGLE WOMEN ARE SAYING

Do you think you would have benefited from being taught about dating? What is the reason for your answer?

- "My choices would have been more educated.... I would have been more selective/cautious when choosing a partner.... I would have waited!"

- "I think I would have made less mistakes if I had the opportunity to really learn from someone."

- "My parents never spoke about relationships. All I knew is that I wasn't supposed to date as a teenager. When I came into adulthood, I was choosing men for all the wrong reasons (cute, nice car, smooth talker, etc.) and had to become mature about my selections through trial and error."

—Single Woman Survey respondents

Chapter Four
LOVE AWAKENED BEFORE ITS TIME

Do not arouse or awaken love until it so desires.

SONG OF SONGS 2:7

I embraced and held tight to the narrative that education was my ticket to freedom and all that life had to offer. I was told I could do anything and be anything I wanted to be if I put my mind to it. Those words were hammered into my head, and believe me when I say that they have stuck with me like glue and that I have focused on my education as if my life depended on it.

My secondary school years were no cakewalk for me. I had to study hard, really hard, to get good grades. I realized very early in my life as a student that a surefire recipe for excelling in my classes and schools as a whole was to read the chapter before class, attend all my classes, take copious notes and later rewrite them in a clean notebook, and consistently study (in groups and alone). I used every available tool to succeed. Truthfully and secretly, I deeply desired to always make my mother proud, and excelling in my education was one tangible way to make her heart smile.

Like most teenagers, when I met a cute boy, I got distracted, my focus on school was sidelined, and my grades began to drop. My infatuation with this boy consumed me, and all else seemed to fade in the background as my young heart became immersed in a hurricane of emotions and daydreams. He lived in the adjoining neighborhood, and we went to the same school. Did I mention he was cute? That captivating smile and those big brown eyes! This cutie met all the requirements of a starry-eyed teenage girl who thought she was in love. I may not have written down that infamous boyfriend list, but honey, he had all the attributes that made this giggly teenager and her friends marvel. As the stereotypical saying goes, "he was tall, dark, and handsome."

We soon became inseparable as a couple at school and in the neighborhood. His exhales were my inhales; he was the yin to my yang. In our teenage minds, we truly loved each other. We walked to school together, ate lunch together under the tamarind tree at school, walked home together, and then spent hours just chatting on the veranda before he continued up the hill to his home.

Our brief separation allowed us to scarf down dinner, skim our homework, and tend to our designated family chores, only to be reunited in the early evening, when we would sit again on the veranda enjoying the cool Caribbean breeze. We would chat and laugh about life and what our future would be like together. We both (well, at least, I did) relished and believed everything we charted out as our life path and future together. It seemed so right and so real.

On school nights, he had to return home early, and I had a bedtime, so we would reluctantly say goodbye as if we were never going to see each other again. Then, like clockwork, I immediately knew that he had safely made the short walk home when the phone began ringing. I would dash to the corner of the living room to answer it so as not to awaken the Farrell household. This call would launch us into another chatting marathon late into the night and the wee hours of the morning. In those days, there was no such thing as call waiting, so all other calls at either end were met with the most annoying busy signal. Our phone conversations always ended with daring each other to be the first to hang up the phone: "You hang up. No, you hang up."

In retrospect, our communications were excessive, but it seemed so natural and necessary. My mother, in all her wisdom and Montserratian dialect, would ask me, "Wat in a de whirl a you ha fi tark bout so?" With the biggest smile on my face, butterflies fluttering in my stomach and a heart filled with joy, I would retort, "We're talking about love." I had never been in love before—this was all so new and exciting to me. In my teenage mind, these feelings were so palpable yet so indescribable.

The inevitable occurred after a few months of this marathon dating situation. In hindsight, I equate it to a head-on collision that was unfolding in full view, but no one cared to intervene or admit it was happening. The result was that my grades for the Easter marking period had significantly plummeted. It was serious enough that my promotion to the fourth form that September was in jeopardy and seemed unlikely. I knew that I wasn't at peak performance in some of my classes, like math, but I was ignorant to the fact that my lower grades would pull down the higher ones. This thing called averages was at play—and math wasn't my strong suit!

The days leading up to me getting my dreaded grades were a mix of anticipation, nervousness, and curiosity. I was uncertain as to how things would turn out and the impact the grades would have on my secondary education. My mind grew restless. Just as time had flown by a few months earlier when I was lovestruck, it now seemed to slow down: each passing moment felt like an eternity.

Finally, it was D-Day, the day that the grades would be posted. Yes, you read that correctly: the grades were going to be publicly posted. This was an embarrassing and sobering reality. In the school system I attended in Montserrat, the teachers were allowed to rank each student from one to whatever number was in that class. Teachers posted the ranking with the students' names outside their classroom door for everyone to see—I mean, everyone.

Needless to say, sleep was elusive that night, and having breakfast the next morning was the furthest thing from my mind. The fear of failing my classes had my stomach in knots and my heart racing. The thought of not being able to advance to the next grade with my friends left me mortified. Even worse was the horror of disappointing my mother. None of my siblings had repeated a grade. I was venturing into uncharted and embarrassing territory.

My sweaty palms clutched my school bag and the tissue that was now mush as I hurried into the open schoolyard and headed for the side entrance to the school building. I was fixed on making my way to my homeroom in one swoop so I could avoid the usual morning pleasantries. With my head down, I made it past the first end of the U-shaped, pale-green-colored building and then the second end. I breathed a sigh of relief, but that was no comfort as I faced two flights of stairs. With all the energy I could muster, I began to climb the seemingly narrow stairs while praying that my feet would not betray me as they landed on each concrete step.

Now at the top of the stairs, I braced myself and approached the door that had the details of my shame plastered to it. I watched as other students crowded around the door, they, too, trying to learn their fate. The class sizes were not big, with no more than twenty students in each class.

I started at the top of the roster and searched for my name in the first ten spots. it wasn't there! My heart sank. I immediately felt the tears welling up in my eyes and blurring my sight, but I continued to work my way down the list. I remember feeling a bit faint, like I was tumbling backward into a deep, dark hole, as I silently and curiously asked myself, as we would say in Montserrat, "how much did I come?" Where did I place in the class?

Before the question could even crystallize, the answer seemed to emerge from the posting. There it was, in a dark blue cursive, my name: Vanessa I. Farrell. It was on the left side of the roster, and my ranking was on the right. I ranked fifteenth out of twenty! I was devastated, I just wanted to disappear right then and there.

Shame and I retraced my steps down those stairs, through that side entrance, and back home. Truth be told, I was never a star student who nailed the first, second, or third spot, but I always passed my classes and never ventured outside a ranking of ten on the infamous, publicly posted class roster.

I was certain that my mother would be sorely disappointed in me and rightly so. I began interrogating myself with a sea of questions that I might have to answer once my public secret was revealed in the privacy of home. How could I have been so negligent? When did my grades start slipping? How did I not know that this was going to happen? What was I going to do? These and other questions buzzed mercilessly in my head as the hot Caribbean sun seemed to pelt its fiery rays at me while I walked home.

I got home from school earlier than usual that day. I busied myself with my normal chores while practicing my responses to my imaginary audience. The guilt was too much to bear, not only for not meeting my own expectations but also for disappointing my mother.

The rhythm within the house shifted as everyone came home. I think they sensed that something was off as my usual bubbly, loud, talkative, life-of-the-party personality was not on display. My mother is a master at sensing a mood shift and would often say to me "your face says it all." She immediately launched into mom mode and wanted to know what was wrong. I asked her if we could talk.

I feared that she was thinking the very worst and that she was silently praying in Montserratian dialect, "Dear Lawd in Heaven, please don't ley dis pickney of mine tell me dat she pregnant—no, no, no, me can't deal with this again!" Her fear was justified and real, having dealt with my older sister becoming a teen mother.

My stomach ached not only from the impending admission of my academic failure but also from the growls and rumblings from hours of food deprivation. I was tired and irritated at myself. I wanted to cry but I had no tears left.

As my mother stood in the kitchen, tending to the contents of the pot for what would be dinner, I broke the news. She stopped stirring the pot, then covered it, interrupting the steam and aroma that filled the air. She turned around and looked at me. For what seemed like an eternity, she said nothing. She was probably silently thanking God that her worst fear was not confirmed.

My mother is a woman of silence and few words, but her face said it all. She looked utterly confused as if she were waiting to hear more while trying to make sense of what she had just heard. Amid the confusion, I could tell she was deeply disappointed.

Then without much fanfare, the expected corporal punishment, or the well-deserved mother's wrath, we sat down at the small dining table. Yet I was careful to sit at arm's length in case there was a sudden shift in the eerie quiet of the room. She seemed to be gathering her thoughts as she stared at me square in the eyes. Her voice was stern with a hint of melody as she said, "Vanessa Ingrid Farrell." The enunciation of my full name was declaration that I had gotten myself into big trouble.

I braced myself for the worst and immediately feared that I was about to lose my lease on love. I silently asked myself: "Would I have to break up with my boyfriend? What would my friends think and say? What about our future hopes and dreams—would they be dashed?" My heart ached at the sheer idea of the anticipated loss.

Then my thoughts were silenced as my mom declared, "It is very clear to everyone that you absolutely cannot serve two masters. So my advice to you is that you need to choose one, *today*!"

It didn't take much for me to understand exactly what she meant and how disappointed she was, but the tug of war between my head and my heart was real and painful. It left me feeling conflicted. My mother did not utter another word to me on the matter, but I knew she would be silently watching me like a hawk.

At the tender age of fifteen, I was suffering from a case of love that was awakened before its time, a love that two teenagers could not sustain while juggling the demands of school, life, and puberty.

I really enjoyed the time my boyfriend and I spent together. I loved to sing, and he loved to dance. In fact, on sunny days, you would find him with a boom box on his shoulder, lugging around a huge piece of cardboard and breakdancing on the streets of our tiny village with his dance crew. We participated in many fun activities with friends. All of this made my teenage years living in Montserrat an exciting and fun time, and I cringed at having to give it all up or even cutting back.

I only had one marking period left in the school year to turn my grades around and regain my footing so I would not be left back in the third form. My boyfriend's grades were not bad, and he was not in jeopardy of not being promoted to the next form. Furthermore, he was less concerned about grades and promotion, as he was on the verge of immigrating to New York City from Montserrat to be reunited with his mother. I was deeply affected by the thought of his upcoming departure and how much I would miss him. However, he reassured me of his unwavering love despite the distance, which brought comfort to my teenage heart.

Nonetheless, I was determined to be promoted to a new form within the secondary school system that coming September. Furthermore, I wanted to enjoy the upcoming summer break at the end of the school year. The thought of repeating a grade would have been a dark cloud looming over the usual sunny, carefree, Caribbean summer days.

Through it all, I was happy that my mother did not forbid me to stop talking to my beloved. However, I clearly heard from this mother-daughter conversation that I needed to make my schoolwork and education my number one priority, and believe me when I say I did. I readjusted my focus, did well in my classes the next semester, and was promoted. However, that conversation of serving only one master and prioritizing my education stuck with me in high school and throughout my college years, perhaps to a fault. I kept my focus steady, and I successfully graduated secondary education, still in love with the same cute boy despite the twists and turns in our relationship.

Somewhere between the fourth and fifth form, my guy relocated to the United States of America. Like many children I knew whose mothers went to America to make a better life for themselves and their kids, my boyfriend, along with his siblings, were reunited with their mother. There I was: a teen in a long-distance relationship, utterly confused about what that really meant. However, we kept in contact through an avalanche of letters, cards, and longingly awaited periodic phone calls. My teenage mind devoured every word and relished the excitement he shared about his new home in America. Everything sounded amazing, fun, and new—flying on a 747 into JFK, riding the trains in the New York City subway, the iconic skyline, winter's first snow fall. I was mesmerized.

I wanted nothing more than to be right there with him. Then, like an answered prayer, and the manifestation of my heart's deepest desire, a few years later my mom, my siblings, and I got our green cards as U.S. residents. Our initial journey took us to St. Croix, in the United States Virgin Islands, but nine months later at age nineteen, I left my family and moved to New York City. Finally, my boyfriend and I we were reunited with high hopes of building a future together. However, our love journey, which is shared in a later chapter, was soon eclipsed by the harsh realities of life and adulting.

Points to Ponder

- Teenage love and the intensity of emotions that come with it can be nostalgic and insightful. Can you relate to the passion and all-consuming feeling of teenage love?
- Remember that teenage love is one of the growing pains of life. It is an opportunity for learning and self-discovery. Embrace the lessons you have learned and the person you have become as a result of those early experiences. Life goes on, and with each new chapter, there are opportunities for love and growth.

WHAT OTHER SINGLE WOMEN ARE SAYING

Do you think you would have benefited from being taught about dating? What is the reason for your answer?

- "If I had been given advice about dating earlier on, it would have possibly prevented me from experiencing a lot of what I didn't want to experience. But I grew up with older West Indian parents who did not believe in talking, much less teaching their children about relationships. The focus was on education and church."

- "It depends what I'm 'taught'—I think I would've benefited more learning sooner to love myself first and honor my sense of worth instead of conforming to societal and cultural norms on how relationships should be."

—Single Woman Survey respondents

Chapter Five
EDUCATION WAS MY GOLDEN TICKET

> Instruct a wise man and he will be wiser still; teach a
> righteous man and he will add to his learning.
>
> PROVERBS 9:9

I remained aware of the potential consequences that my poor academic performance in high school had posed to my fourth-form promotion. This experience served as a constant reminder of what it felt like to fail and, more important, what it meant if I failed.

I knew that failing academically would jeopardize my chances of achieving the life I so desired. It would mean settling for mediocre jobs, struggling to pay bills, and constantly feeling unfulfilled. I could not bear the thought of wasting my God-given potential and not living up to expectations that I held for myself, not to mention, my mother.

I graduated high school at eighteen. That same year, my family emigrated from Montserrat to St. Croix, United States Virgin Islands. Nine months later, I relocated to New York and reunited with my high school sweetheart.

The next few years were fun-filled. I rekindled my friendship with my sweetheart, explored every nook and cranny of the Big Apple, and settled into my new job and home. It was an such exciting time for me; everything felt novel and unfamiliar. I was constantly amazed at the vibrancy of the city and its diversity of people. I marveled at the towering skyscrapers that seemed to reach the heavens, the bustling streets, and fast-moving subway trains. This was a far cry from the serenity of my homeland of Montserrat with its tranquil beaches, lush green landscapes, and unhurried, friendly people.

The seasons quickly changed, and I eagerly awaited my first snowfall, which blanketed New York City with four inches on Thanksgiving of 1989. This was a record-breaking event since the city hadn't seen snow on Thanksgiving Day since 1938. It was a captivating and enchanting sight, bringing to life what I had only seen in movies and photographs until now. Despite the freezing temperature, my boyfriend and I frolicked in the snow and enjoyed the sudden and magical transformation of a concrete jungle into a winter wonderland. I vividly remember the moment when I moved my hand out of the cozy comfort of my glove and reached out to catch the soft, cold snowflakes. I watched in glee as they gently gathered in my palm only to quickly melt away. The beauty that surrounded me left me in awe, and a childlike joy and delight instantly filled my heart.

Despite my enjoyment of my new home and dating life, the pursuit of higher education always lingered in the background. I didn't want to have a significant gap between high school and college, as I feared forgetting important academic knowledge and dreaded the thought of being in class with peers much younger than me.

Finally, at age twenty-two, I made the decision to enroll in college part time. I had a grand vision of my boyfriend joining me on this educational journey, but my efforts to convince him were in vain. Undeterred, I embarked on this solo adventure with a clear vision for my life. I was determined to pursue my education as if my life depended on it because, in many ways, it truly did.

My excitement about starting college quickly turned into disappointment when I was informed that I needed to complete a semester of remedial classes to demonstrate my readiness for college. It was a harsh realization that my Caribbean Examination Council and Cambridge O Levels, which had indicated my successful completion of secondary school in Montserrat, were not considered equivalent to a high school diploma in the United States. This revelation was not only embarrassing, but it was also distressing, especially considering the effort I had put into addressing this very issue by earning a GED while living on St. Croix.

I was taken aback and caught off guard, feeling as though I had been blindsided. In retrospect, I can see that I was unfairly treated due to my Caribbean schooling. The idea of having to spend money I didn't have and an entire semester proving my proficiency in basic subjects like math, English, and reading infuriated me. I was determined to challenge this policy, so I advocated for myself and was eventually given the chance to test out of these remedial classes.

The day of reckoning had arrived. It was the moment that would determine whether I would be labeled as a remedial or conventional college student. To ensure I had ample time to prepare and avoid feeling rushed, I took the entire day off from work. I woke up slightly earlier than usual but only found myself trying to calm the butterflies that fluttered incessantly in my stomach. Uncertainty hung over me as I hadn't been exactly sure what to study for. This uneasiness left every nerve in my body on edge as if I were standing on the precipice of a great unknown.

I hurriedly made my way from my apartment to the nearby bus stop, the bustling streets of my Brooklyn neighborhood adding an extra layer of exhaustion to my already anxious state. I dodged traffic, maneuvered around the familiar panhandler, and navigated the crowded sidewalks. The bus arrived just in time, its brakes hissing as the doors swung open, offering a temporary respite from the chaotic streets.

I found a seat toward the back of the bus, settling in as it pulled away from the curb. The bus ride felt like a blur. Finally, the bus came to a stop, and I joined the stream of people disembarking onto the busy sidewalk. The testing location loomed in the distance, an unassuming building that held the promise of both challenge and opportunity.

As I stepped into the classroom, my heart raced in my chest, its beats echoing in my ears. I quickly scanned the room filled with unfamiliar faces and sensed that there was a collective nervousness silently lurking in the air.

Choosing a seat in the front row, I settled on the far-right side near a bank of louvered windows. The sturdy desk-and-chair combo provided a sense of stability as I placed my bag on the floor. Taking a deep breath, I whispered a prayer, ready to give it my all. I knew that this was an opportunity to prove to myself that I could overcome this obstacle, too.

In less than a week, the results would be available, determining which classes I would be able to take that semester. As days passed by, a sense of eerie déjà vu settled in the pit of my stomach, taking me back to that high school experience when I had failed so miserably. Now in the United States, I aimlessly paced the floor of my apartment, desperately trying to recall the test questions and how I had answered them.

With a mix of anticipation and trepidation, I made my way to my college counselor's office to collect my test results. When I entered her office, my counselor's expression was unreadable, offering no clues as to what awaited me. The room was quiet, the air heavy with the weight of uncertainty.

She handed me the envelope, and I held my breath as I tore it open. My eyes scanned the page, disbelief washing over me. I glanced up at my counselor, noticing an immediate shift in her demeanor. Our eyes met, and she offered a warm smile before moving behind the large wooden desk, gently patting me on the shoulder. I had not only passed all three categories of the test, but I had also excelled beyond my wildest dreams. A surge of emotion welled up inside me, threatening to burst forth. Unable to contain my joy, I scrambled to retrieve a crumpled Kleenex from my purse, but it was no match for the hot tears that streamed down my face.

At that moment, time seemed to slip away from me, but I gathered my composure, offered my gratitude and appreciation to my counselor, and carefully exited her office, allowing space for other students who anxiously awaited their fate. The overwhelming feeling of accomplishment washed over me, bringing a deep sense of satisfaction that validated all of my hard work and self-advocacy.

In that moment, I realized that I had proven myself. I had overcome the obstacles and doubts that had plagued me, and I had emerged victorious. The journey had been challenging, but the reward was sweet. With renewed confidence, I knew that I could achieve anything I set my mind to.

While working full time, I wholeheartedly dedicated myself to pursuing my college degree. Unfortunately, a few years later, in my mid-twenties, my relationship with my boyfriend ended—a significant life experience that I will delve into in a later chapter.

Undeterred, I immersed myself in my studies, diligently poring over textbooks and taking meticulous notes. Whenever I needed clarification or guidance, I sought help without hesitation from teachers, librarians, and peers.

I pulled countless all-nighters and spent entire weekends in the library, taking breaks only to shop for groceries, do laundry, or attend church on Sundays. I pushed myself to the limit, refusing to put myself "out there" as being single and available and sacrificing any meaningful dating opportunities that could potentially lead to a serious relationship. My college classes became my top priority, causing me to forgo social outings and leisure activities to stay focused.

The journey was far from easy: there were tons of tears and persistent prayers. Doubt often crept in as I questioned whether all my efforts would be worth it. But I quickly reminded myself of the alternative—a life of regret and missed opportunities. Giving up was never an option. There were days when I felt alone and lonely, longing for my family back home in the Caribbean and yearning to have the familiarity of my boyfriend by my side. I watched enviously as my friends enjoyed the pleasures of dating, forming relationships, getting married, and starting families.

As the years went by, my hard work began to pay off. I excelled in college, and my passion for my chosen profession grew stronger with each passing day. The fear of failure slowly transformed into a burning desire for success. I became hungry for knowledge, eager to prove to myself and others that I could achieve greatness. Looking back on these pivotal moments in my life, I am grateful for the fear of failure that pushed me to become the person I am today. This fear taught me resilience, humility, and the power of a strong work ethic.

I am no longer afraid of failure; instead, I see it as an opportunity for growth and self-improvement.

Throughout my college career, I was intentional in seeking wisdom and mentorship from successful Black women who shared my drive for education and career advancement. These trailblazers were breaking barriers in various fields, holding esteemed positions, running nonprofits and consultancies, and even venturing into entrepreneurship. They excelled in professions such as education, law, health care, and research.

I observed the traits these women had in common and noticed how they navigated challenges with grace. Their unwavering commitment to education stood out as they achieved secondary school completion and pursued higher degrees. Some were married with children though most were not. I greatly admired their courage, strength, and fearlessness, and I aspired to follow in their footsteps.

When I was twenty-eight, I proudly earned my bachelor's degree in health and nutrition sciences. This was a significant achievement for me, as it marked the culmination of years of hard work and dedication. But I didn't stop there. At age thirty, I went on to earn my master's degree in public health, receiving the department's Helen Sloan Award, a prestigious recognition given to outstanding students who have demonstrated exceptional academic achievement and a commitment to community service.

In that same year, I decided to take a leap of faith and apply for a fellowship program at the prestigious Centers for Disease Control and Prevention (CDC). Despite being warned about the fierce competition and the difficulty of securing a position at such an esteemed institution, I pressed on to my delight, I was accepted into the program, a moment that stands out as a highlight of my public health career.

In the years that followed, I continued to push myself and achieve new milestones. I became a Master Certified Health Education Specialist and a Certified Health Coach, further expanding my knowledge and skill set. These certifications opened doors to a wide range of opportunities, allowing me to work in various capacities and assume leadership roles. More recently, I made the bold decision to venture into full-time entrepreneurship. I established my own health coaching and consulting practice, giving me a platform for sharing my expertise and for making a meaningful impact on the lives of others.

Truth be told, the road was not smooth, and I learned so much more from what was not written on the pages of my textbooks, lessons that have shaped my knowledge, life path, and choices.

I feel compelled to share my journey of acquiring my educational and professional accomplishments for a specific reason. Looking back, I can now clearly see how, like the resilient "strong Black women" in my life who courageously raised their children alone and hammered into my head the importance of education, I have also mirrored some of these lessons in nurturing my own educational pursuits. Expressing this sentiment is not easy, as it requires confronting and articulating deep emotions. It is even more challenging to put these feelings into words, as they are raw and vulnerable. However, as I earned each degree, I felt like I was birthing my own babies, but it came at the cost of sacrificing my future love life and long-term relationships.

Each delivery required dedication, hard work, and countless sacrifices. There were moments when I questioned whether it was all worth it, but deep down, I knew that education held the key to unlocking my potential and achieving my dreams. Each milestone I reached brought a sense of accomplishment and pride. Whether it was acing a difficult exam or receiving recognition for my achievements, those moments made all the late nights and early mornings worth it. They fueled my determination to keep pushing forward, even when the road ahead seemed daunting.

Needless to say, with every step I took toward academic success, I couldn't help but notice the toll it was taking on other aspects of my life. The countless hours spent studying and preparing for exams meant less time for socializing and building meaningful relationships. It felt like a constant juggling act, trying to balance my academic pursuits with my desire for a well-rounded life. And then there were the physical sacrifices. Sitting for hours on end, hunched over textbooks or in front of a computer screen, took a toll on my body. I often found myself neglecting exercise and self-care, prioritizing my studies above all else. It was a trade-off I made, knowing that my education was a priority, but this trade-off wasn't without consequences.

My educational journey was a double-edged sword. It brought me immense personal growth and opened doors to opportunities I never thought possible. But it also came at a cost—a cost that I was willing to pay but one that I cannot ignore. I have made some major personal sacrifices on my educational journey. I find that it's important to acknowledge and reflect on these experiences, as they shape who I am and what I value. Education is a powerful tool, but looking back it's essential to find a balance that allows for thriving academically while nurturing one's social and physical well-being.

As a lifelong learner, I seek to keep current in my profession, but I am vigilant about taking a step back and evaluating the social impact it has on my life. My goal is to strive for success but not at the expense of my happiness and overall well-being. After all, true fulfillment comes from finding harmony in all aspects of life—academic, professional, social, and physical.

I now realize that my perspective on dating and education was very limited and rigid. I believed that I had to sacrifice one for the other, but I have come to understand that they can coexist and complement each other. Instead of viewing dating as a distraction, I see it as an opportunity for personal growth and connection. It is indeed possible to have a fulfilling romantic life while still pursuing my personal and professional goals.

Points to Ponder

- For women raised by single mothers and even more so in the Black community, where women are often the head of the household, education is hailed as the golden ticket!
- Remember to create a more balanced and holistic approach to your life. There is no need to choose between having a fulfilling love or dating life and your professional pursuits. You should strive to embrace both aspects of your life and to find joy and fulfillment in each as they have the power to support and enhance each other.

WHAT OTHER SINGLE WOMEN ARE SAYING

Do you desire to be married in the future? If your answer is no, please state your reason.

- "I have been hurt emotionally, physically, and mentally too many times; therefore, I do not trust men and will not allow anybody to get close to me ever again."

- "I am afraid."

- "I don't want to be married because society says that I should be or what others expect of me. I don't want to get married to be unhappy. I don't want to get married to put in more work than the other person. I believe that we must make equal sacrifices."

- "In today's society with such betrayal and lack of loyalty to spouse and family, it's best to have my sanity."

—Single Woman Survey respondents

Chapter Six
SORRY CAN'T COOL IT!

> Be kind and compassionate to one another, forgiving
> each other, just like in Christ God forgave you.
>
> EPHESIANS 4:32

I used to think forgiveness was giving someone else a free pass for their indiscretions toward me. This was etched so deeply into my brain that sometimes I would not entertain matters of forgiveness with myself or anyone else—especially the perpetrator. I had the one-sided mindset that everything a person did to me was intentional, maliciously planned, and orchestrated against me. I never considered that I may have caused hurt and pain or imposed some thoughtlessness, known or unknown, on other people whom I hoped would forgive me.

At first glance, forgiveness may appear to be simple and straightforward. However, the act of forgiving is undoubtedly one of the most unnerving, challenging, and life-altering experiences a human will ever confront. I have been guilty of dismissing the requests of others who wanted me to forgive them, while on the other hand, I have found myself festering in a cesspool of feeling misunderstood when I wasn't given an exemption for my carelessness and transgressions. I could not reconcile why another couldn't see that I had simply made a mistake or had just misspoken. It was challenging to comprehend why others found it difficult to forgive me. I wanted so desperately from others what I was unwilling to give them in return.

Therein lies the problem.

I have come to understand that forgiveness is a learned skill: it is more of an art than a science, and people have varying viewpoints on the issue. Forgiveness is neither absolute nor black and white. It is a learned behavior that we develop over time. If we are alive and are in relationship with others, we will find ourselves on both ends of the spectrum as either the forgiver or the forgiven.

When I grew up in the Caribbean in a single-mother household, forgiveness was never a focused topic of conversation—at least not in our house. Our stance on forgiveness was extremely watered down. It was limited to my mother or a teacher or some other adult demanding that I "say sorry" to my sister, brother, cousin, friend, or classmate whom I had offended. Occasionally, there was a brave soul in the pack who would shout in protest, "Sorry can't cool it." Nonetheless, someone's plea for forgiveness was so diluted and mechanical that it might as well have never happened—but in a child's mind, hearing the word "sorry" was enough. In a matter of days, hours, or even minutes, we would be back in each other's company and as thick as thieves with the offender without any concerns or deliberation about the pain and hurt that had just been inflicted.

Unknowingly, I have dragged these patterns of superficial forgiveness into adulthood, life, relationships, and especially the arena of love. Over time, I have learned that this kindergarten strategy of forgiveness—the one that kept our childhood friendships intact, the one we have basically rinsed and repeated hundreds of times over the years—is highly flawed, weak, and unsustainable. I have come to realize that forgiveness goes much further than saying "I am sorry." Instead, you need time to talk the situation through and to express your feelings, emotions, and anger. If you are in a real adult relationship, you may find yourself discussing ways to mitigate those negative behaviors for the good of the relationship and for the well-being of each person involved.

In my adult dating experiences, I have been guilty of accepting the mindless rendering of "I am sorry" for indiscretions that were destined to be the demise of the relationship. In my early years of dating, I still used the kindergarten forgiveness strategy, and I accepted it from the men I dated. I never talked about or dug more deeply into things that bothered me for fear of rocking the boat or having the relationship end in an untimely way. To this day, I wish I had spoken up more and asked the right questions when I felt offended by the actions of the men I dated. On the other hand, I had to be willing to accept and offer forgiveness in a meaningful and mature way whenever I was the perpetrator of the crime. I failed to realize that dating was a time for data gathering and that asking the right questions was paramount. Having these conversations is an essential part of the dating experience. This might be surprising to those who know me because I am very vocal and outspoken. However, this trait lay dormant during my early years of dating. Honestly, I struggled in this area because I found out early that asking questions seemed to offend most men and left me feeling like I had committed a crime.

As I look back over my dating experiences, I can clearly recognize how some of these patterns of ill behaviors were shaped and perpetuated. This was evident when my high school sweetheart cheated on me, and I forgave him because he said he was sorry. Then he cheated again, and I forgave him because, again, he said he was sorry. We never sat down to have a real conversation about why he thought his behavior was acceptable. What's worse is that I never asked myself why I continuously accepted such mistreatment.

With this pattern of betrayal and forgiveness so ingrained in the relationship, I am certain he thought that the final straw handed to me on a balmy Mother's Day (of all days) would not affect our relationship. Yes, he confessed that once again he had cheated, but this time the betrayal was evident not only to me but to the entire world. He had shamelessly fathered a child with another woman.

His plea for forgiveness came like clockwork, but on this Sunday morning, it was delivered with a bit of drama, one worthy of an Oscar nomination.

"I'm sorry, Vanny," he said. "I don't know how it happened."

I felt sucker punched. Had I heard what I thought I had heard? His claim that he didn't "know how it happened" left me confused and angry. I scoffed at his effort to insult my intelligence—since it was clear that the science of reproduction had not changed since my last biology class.

Despite all the drama, disappointment, and sense of impending doom surrounding me and this relationship, believe it or not, I felt genuinely sorry for him. Then, just as I had done so many times before, I did what I had grown accustomed to and stayed in the relationship. However, this time, something felt different: I found it extremely difficult to forgive him fully and genuinely. I couldn't reconcile his behavior or sweep it under the rug this time because the evidence of his betrayal was very much alive: it was breathing, and it would grow up.

After a year of festering emotions and dying to myself daily, I decided I had to forgive and just let it go. The pain was real, and I felt that at any given moment I would explode from the anger, the fear, and the resentment that were brewing inside of me. A dark cloud had enveloped my life; it was a constant companion that followed me to work daily and forced me to retreat to my bed for hours. Life seemed hopeless. I felt like someone had broken into my home and stolen my joy and my peace, and the ransom being demanded was forgiveness. I struggled to accept forgiveness as something I could truly offer. My head and my heart could not resolve the betrayal, and the repeating soundtrack of my mind was "How can I sincerely forgive him after he has done this terrible thing to me?"

Then, without warning, a shift took place within me, redirecting my attention away from my own anguish and toward the actions and behaviors of my boyfriend. I became intrigued to discover if his transgression was impacting him in the same way it had affected me. To my surprise, I noticed how skillfully he had managed to separate his roles as a new father and a boyfriend, ensuring that his two worlds did not collide. Although I took on my role as a citizen scientist without any specific expectation, I ultimately gained a profound life lesson from my observation. I learned that forgiveness does not hinge on the action or awareness of the offender, as the offender may carry on without remorse or knowledge of the pain he has inflicted. Instead, I discovered that forgiveness is a deeply personal journey centered on my own growth and healing.

I was young, only twenty-five years old at the time, and had much to live for. My happiness could not be based on someone else's behavior. So, with all the energy I could muster, I decided to have a heartfelt conversation with my boyfriend about how I was feeling and my decision to honestly forgive him.

I had rehearsed and prayed about the impending conversation in my head more times than I care to admit, and I was ready for whatever the outcome was. Well, that's a lie—I wasn't ready—but it was a conversation that needed to happen sooner rather than later. The shame of the situation was real, and it was eating me alive.

It was a Tuesday evening. We had both survived the business of navigating the streets and transportation system of New York City, a maddening feat that I have never really acclimated to. The world was still buzzing outside as we stood facing each other in the solitude and quiet of my ground-floor Brooklyn apartment. The air was filled with a combination of anticipation and nervousness as his six-foot frame towered over me, evoking a strange mix of familial tenderness and tension.

Like old times, it was just the two of us, but instead of our favorite songbird, Anita Baker, chirping in the background, coupled with our easy embrace and sweet small talk, the air was thick, punctuated only by the sound of our breathing and the occasional sigh. We were both fully aware that this very moment would cause a monumental shift in our relationship as we decided whether we would stay together or chart solo journeys of healing and forgiveness. It was a long-overdue conversation, one we needed to have.

Since I had requested the meeting, it was only fair that I deliver my thoughts first, so I braced myself and launched into my planned comments. Despite my rehearsal, I was a mess, and without warning, an avalanche of emotions washed over me. I was anxious, afraid, angry, and sad. Still, as silly as this may sound, I also felt empathy for my boyfriend; in my heart, I think he was truly sorry for his actions. On the other hand, a part of me wondered if his transgression were less visible in the court of public opinion, would we be standing here tonight?

The tears streamed down my face, and my voice began to crack. This seemed to him like the perfect opportunity to hijack the conversation.

He held my hands, and I looked up at him, willing myself to ignore those big, brown, dreamy eyes. Then he began with the usual, all-too-familiar, kindergarten plea for forgiveness.

"I am sorry, Vanny," he said. I had heard him utter that expression so many times. "I am sorry."

I was vexed. I was tired of the same old mantra. I needed to reclaim the conversation. I wanted to give voice to my feelings, to break the silence I had endured for the past year.

I took a deep breath, and in my calmest voice, I interrupted him.

"If the situation were reversed, would you forgive me?"

The moment this question left my lips, the conversation shifted in a way that knocked the wind out of my sails.

"No."

I stood frozen as I heard his answer again in my mind: "No."

His heartbreaking response—that he would not forgive me in the same situation—unleashed a range of intense emotions that I did not know could coexist all at a given time in one human being. I was shocked with an overwhelming sense of disbelief, stunned and unable to fully comprehend what had just happened. I felt betrayed, as his response was contrary to my expectations. It seemed so easy for him to expect so freely from me what he vehemently refused to offer in return. My anguish was a mix of sadness, anger, confusion, and a profound sense of loss. Even though it was clear that I needed to end the relationship, I was losing my best friend of ten years, and it was a challenging reality. I was disappointed. The hopes and dreams of what could have been shattered before me.

Most difficult of all was the deep feeling of vulnerability that engulfed me. My walls of protection were crumbling, falling away because they were built on sand that shifted every time there was an act of transgression and I decided to stay in the relationship. Here we were years later, and I was left feeling raw and exposed.

His heart-wrenching response was my cue to leave the relationship and truly forgive, forget, and let go. And with that, a decade-long love relationship unceremoniously ended that Tuesday evening.

The days and weeks that followed were tough, full of mixed emotions and self-doubt. I questioned whether I had made the right decision to leave and wondered what life would be like as a single woman not in a relationship.

I told my family and a few mutual friends what had transpired and my decision to end the relationship. While most of them understood, there were some who had grown up with us who seemed to be still living vicariously through us and had high hopes for our relationship. They were disheartened. But through it all, I was resolved in my decision.

My circle of friends had grown over the years, but close ties to my Caribbean roots never wavered. Having those familiar family and close friends by my side during this time was incredibly important for me in terms of emotional support. They offered me a shoulder to cry on and a listening ear, providing comfort and reassurance. Their presence gave me a different perspective and validated my feelings, understanding my pain and empathizing with what I was going through. The moments of distraction from the breakup pain that they provided brought a bit of joy and laughter into my life. I welcomed those unexpected flashes of nostalgia when I was in the circle of my people; from the dialect that required no translation to foods that needed no labels. Most importantly, I was grateful to God that I had my own place and not have to worry about that aspect of my life, but I knew I could depend on these individuals if the need arose. Their presence not only offered comfort and guidance but also a sense of belonging during this challenging time.

By God's grace, I slowly began feeling like myself again. For me, being able to truly forgive meant that I no longer felt drained and tired from holding on to the pain and being resentful. Time spent thinking about the experience dwindled, and my focus turned to me. I felt a sense of relief, as things felt more peaceful in my home and in my heart. It was liberating, a feeling that one year earlier I never would have been able to imagine.

I had honestly forgiven him, and most important, I had forgiven myself. I forgave myself for allowing my heart to be trampled on. I forgave myself. I am grateful to God for the strength to follow his prompting even if at the time other forces seemed stronger.

Points to Ponder

- As you reflect on your childhood experiences, you may notice patterns of your childhood forgiveness strategy playing out in your adult love relationships. Forgiveness does not mean accepting or condoning harmful behavior: it means choosing to let go of the negative emotions and moving forward with love and compassion for yourself and others.

- Remember that forgiveness is not about the other person—it is a gift you give freely to yourself. In order to live a life of joy and happiness, it is necessary to let go of any transgressions, whether they are inflicted by you or others. Holding onto grudges or resentment only weighs you down and hinders your ability to move forward.

WHAT OTHER SINGLE WOMEN ARE SAYING

Do you desire to be married in the future? If your answer is "yes" or "maybe," do you have an ideal age at which you would like to be married?

- "When I was younger, I thought I would be married between twenty-seven and thirty. Now that I am over thirty, I am more focused on having the right man by my side rather than the actual age I will get married. Life is a journey. There are no deadlines or timelines written in stone to accomplish certain milestones that we must abide by. When the time is right, it will happen. Until then, being happy is my main focus right now."

- "NOW! (Sixty-five years old) Not getting any younger."

—Single Woman Survey respondents

Chapter Seven
THE INVISIBLE CLOCK

He settles the childless woman in her home as a happy mother of children.

PSALMS 113:9

Unlike men, women have a limited window of time for what is considered a viable pregnancy. This biological reality often drives many women's desires for partnership and marriage. This is completely understandable. As the clock ticks closer to the eleventh hour (a woman's mid-forties), various insecurities start to consume us if we don't have a partner, marriage, or the prospect of having a baby. Even if we have no desire for children, society has a knack for making us feel inadequate as women if we haven't checked off these societal expectations.

For many single women, the desire to become a mother can be all-consuming and overwhelming. It can become the pebble in our shoe that distracts us from reality and clouds our judgment when it comes to choosing a suitable partner for marriage and fatherhood. These desires are real and undeniable, but it is important to manage them carefully and not let them lead us to make choices that go against God's intended order.

In my early adulthood, I made a firm decision for myself and a promise to God: "No husband, no baby!" Despite my resolve, there were the well-meaning women who rendered their advice and urged me to have a child as if it were a simple decision. They would say things like "girl, you should just have a child" or "go ahead, have just one" or "have one, at least you'll have your 'own' child." Shockingly, I have also been accused of being selfish for not having a child. But bringing a child into the world is a serious matter; it's not as if you are buying a dress that can be returned if it doesn't suit your liking. Neither the advice nor the accusation resonates with me.

I also witnessed the struggles of my friends and other women who found themselves pregnant and abandoned by the men they loved and trusted. It stirred a complex mix of emotions within me—empathy for their vulnerability, anger toward the offenders, and as a witness, a profound sense of helplessness. It broke my heart to see my friends put their dreams on hold to care for their child.

I understood that being married does not guarantee a stable relationship or automatic support after childbirth. However, having grown up with a single mother, I also knew the challenges and hardships that could come with raising a child alone. I understood the immense responsibility and sacrifice that would be required. I chose the path of "no husband, no baby" to avoid unnecessary stress and hardship. The thought of struggling through life as a single mother and having the weight of another person's survival on my shoulders was a daunting prospect.

Whether it is societal pressure or biological instinct, many women experience what is commonly referred to as "baby fever." This is a strong desire to have a child, even if the circumstances may not be ideal. I remember feeling this way in my late twenties, despite being single and knowing that it was not the right time for me to have a child. It was confusing and difficult to make sense of these conflicting emotions.

I sought advice from a colleague who was also a nurse, and she reassured me that these feelings were normal. However, I made a conscious decision to not let these thoughts linger and to stick to my resolve: "no husband, no baby." I knew that it was important to prioritize having the right partner and creating a stable foundation for a family before embarking on motherhood.

As I made my way through my potential childbearing years, I could not help but feel a deep sense of fulfillment and accomplishment at the way that my life was unfolding. I had checked off all the boxes that society told me I needed to meet the quintessential markers of success: I had avoided becoming a teenager mother, and I had completed my education, bought a home, and built a successful career.

Now, at age thirty-five, I arrived at my gynecologist's office for a routine annual visit. The receptionist greeted me with a warm smile as I signed in and took a seat. After what felt like an eternity, the nurse called my name. I followed her down the hallway, noticing the sound of my footsteps echoing off the sterile walls. We entered the examination room, and I took a seat on the cold, paper-covered table. The nurse left, promising that the doctor would be with me shortly.

Finally, there was a soft knock, followed by my doctor's entrance into the room. His usually warm smile had been replaced with a serious expression. He sat down across from me, flipping open a file. I could feel my heart rate quicken, a sense of unease settling in the pit of my stomach.

Our eyes met, and I could see a concerned look in his gaze. I mustered up the courage to ask if something was wrong. My words came out in a trembling voice, betraying my anxiety. I searched his face for any hint of reassurance, but he seemed lost in thought, searching for the right words. A heavy silence hung in the air as he took a deep breath. Finally, he spoke, his voice measured and calm.

"Vanessa, you are approaching a critical stage in your reproductive years," he began. "As you know, the window of viable pregnancy becomes narrower as you get older."

His words hit me like a ton of bricks, and my mind started racing. All I could hear was the ticking of my so-called biological clock, the sudden pressure to find a partner, get married, and start a family before it was too late. The room seemed to spin, and I instinctively gripped the edge of the examination table, trying to steady myself and regain my balance.

What he said was undeniably true. But I found myself becoming defensive and thinking of counterarguments. I thought about women I knew who had healthy babies in their late forties, and I reminded myself of the promise I had made to God "no husband, no baby." I also held onto the belief that if it was God's will for me to be a mother, it would happen.

I voiced my thoughts to my doctor. He listened attentively and acknowledged that there were indeed women who had successful pregnancies in their late forties. Then without pausing for a moment, he layered on a dose of reality.

"You might see the result of a beautiful baby," he said, "but for each successful pregnancy, there are numerous heart-wrenching stories of women who waited too long."

He paused, making sure his words were sinking in.

"These women face infertility and other challenges that rob them of the dream of motherhood."

He bent his head, then looked up at me again. "This is the toughest part of my job," he said.

It was a sobering reality check. But it did not change the fact that I was nowhere close to entertaining the thought of having a child; most important, I was single, and I had no prospect of marriage in sight.

In his attempt to cover all the bases, he looked up from writing in my file, tilted his gaze, and asked, "Have you considered sperm donation or artificial insemination?"

The question caught me off guard, and I suddenly felt exposed. While the idea of having a baby wasn't at the forefront of my mind, I couldn't help but wonder if this was my only option for motherhood. The conversation quickly became heavy and uncomfortable, and I immediately responded with a firm "no."

My abrupt response was based on my upbringing and personal beliefs. It wasn't a judgment on the practice itself but rather a response shaped by my familial, cultural, and religious values. Growing up, I had limited knowledge about sperm donation and artificial insemination. These topics were rarely discussed, and I had never personally encountered anyone who had had a baby through these methods. It was a completely new concept to me until I moved to the United States. While I cannot totally deny the possibility of babies being conceived through this method during that time, I was completely unaware of such occurrences. However, what I did witness were occasional pregnancies and births where the father's identity remained unknown. These situations were likely a result of secretive relationships, unrelated to women seeking artificial insemination with a sperm donor. It was not my place, nor that of the other villagers, to meddle into these matters.

As my doctor and I wrapped up our conversation, I found myself thinking out loud.

"Furthermore," I said before I could tame my thoughts or my tongue, "this sperm donor thing would just totally confuse my grandmother!"

He raised his head from writing his note and smiled. Both of us enjoyed a good chuckle.

I gathered my things and my thoughts. I left that appointment a bit pensive, but I was resolved in my decision to just wait on God's timing and His plan for my life.

This was not the end of the talks about the invisible ticking clock and the baby-making conversations, both with myself and others over the years. More times than I care to recall, the question "why don't you have children?" was a dagger directed at me from many sources and many suitors. At times I would become overly sensitive or would even retreat when I was confronted with this question. Over time, I was able to be less reactive to this query. I knew that whether I became a mother or not, I was not defined by my parental status, and moreover, I knew this situation was way beyond my control.

I didn't know how my life would turn out and whether motherhood was in my stars, but I stayed hopeful in the face of the unknown. Through it all, I was very clear that my womanhood was not defined by whether I had a child. Not having a child did not make me less of a woman or a whole person. Birthing a child would not in any way solidify my standing as a contributing member of society, and I refused to be shamed about not having a child. What's more, I truly believe that over the years I have been able to serve as a mother to so many children whom I didn't give birth to. My mothering came in the role of being a godmother, auntie, cousin, mentor, and a friend. Additionally, since 2015, I have been a child-sponsor to an amazing young man who lives in Rwanda, Africa through Compassion International, a Christian charity organization. I have and will continue to pour love and attention into the lives of young people. Through it all, I have kept the faith, knowing fully in my heart that whatever the outcome, biological child or not, I would be content.

Points to Ponder

- Are you a woman with no children? How do you find comfort in a society that places such value on motherhood while silently stigmatizing and judging the childless woman?

- Remember that you are valuable, worthy, and deserving of love and respect, regardless of your marital or parental status. Your worth is not defined by societal expectations but by the inherent value you possess as a human being. Trust in God's plan and believe that He has a purpose for you, no matter the time displayed on your biological clock. Seek guidance and peace through prayer, meditation, or spiritual practices that bring you comfort.

WHAT OTHER SINGLE WOMEN ARE SAYING

What do you do to put yourself out there to find a mate?

- "Right now, nothing special. But in the past, I have tried dating websites, speed dating, and attending singles events. A friend tries to set me up sometimes (it's her hobby, setting up people!). Now I just live my life and talk to people. I think my church should do more activities to help people meet and marry."

- "Whenever I am out in public, I dress very feminine and classy (like I am someone's future wife). I would go to places by myself that have men who are potential mates, for example, a bar, nice restaurant, etc."

—Single Woman Survey respondents

Chapter Eight
JUGGLING THE BOYS

> Charm is deceptive, and beauty is fleeting; but a
> woman who fears the Lord is to be praised.
>
> PROVERBS 31:30

As my college years were winding down, it seemed like I was constantly being set up on blind dates by people I knew or who knew of me. Whether it was a son, a brother, a cousin, or a friend of a friend, there was always someone they wanted me to meet, convinced that he was the perfect match for me. Initially, I was flattered and excited by the prospect of meeting new people and potentially finding love. However, there were moments when I couldn't help but feel like a project, as if I needed to be fixed up with someone to be complete. At times, these dating experiences left me feeling hopeless and exhausted.

Initially, the concept of being set up on a blind date or going on one seemed completely foreign to me. It was something I had only seen portrayed on television or read about in books. However, since moving to America from the Caribbean, I had heard a few women mention that they had met their significant other through a blind date. In my mind, it almost seemed like a fairy tale.

To truly understand my perspective, it is important to consider the cultural background in which I was raised. Blind dates simply did not exist in our culture, and people did not partake in them. If they did do so, I was not privy to it. Our community was so small that it was highly unlikely to encounter someone you did not already know. The process of dating was straightforward: a boy would notice a girl, develop an interest, engage in small talk, and gradually increase his interactions with her. Eventually, the boy and the girl would become an item, and they might end up marrying or having a few children together. This simplistic approach to relationships often left many women feeling chosen but without the opportunity to actively choose a mate for themselves.

Despite my initial uneasiness, I approached the experience of blind dates with an open mind. There was always a feeling of enthusiasm and suspense in meeting someone for the first time. Being rusty in the dating department, I saw this as an opportunity to practice and sharpen my dating skills. I told myself that it was a chance to meet new people I would have never otherwise crossed paths with.

While these dating experiences did give me the opportunity to meet some incredible men and form a few lifelong friendships, many of my blind dates seemed to carry a common rhythm in the way they unfolded. The dates were often filled with anticipation, nerves, and hope yet were also frequently veiled with uncertainty and unpredictability. Some of the blind dates turned out to be fun and memorable, while others were forgettable.

Each date was unique and exposed me to new and interesting places, culinary delights, and cultures, expanding my horizons and my appreciation for whatever city I called home at the time.

As time went on, I began to learn more about myself and my quirks, what I liked and what I needed to work on. Additionally, I started to recognize and admire qualities that I found attractive in a potential partner and those that repelled me.

While in the dating arena, I puckered up and smooched my fair share of frogs. But unfortunately, not even one of those amphibians transformed into my Prince Charming. As I muse over my past dating escapades, there are times when I find myself being all too human and dissecting my dating demise and dilemmas. I can't help but wonder if I could have done things differently. Did a potential suitor slip through my fingers or me theirs?

The questions in my head were relentless. Was my self-confidence so low that it could be measured in negative numbers? Or on the other hand, was it so high that I came off overly confident? Did I exude insecurity like a neon sign? Or did I radiate a sense of self-assurance and grace? Did I fail to recognize my worth as a fabulous woman in this crazy world? Or did I possess a humble confidence that drew others toward me? Did I struggle to articulate my values and establish boundaries while navigating the treacherous waters of dating? Or did I assert my needs and set healthy boundaries, ensuring my own emotional well-being? And last, was I just plain immature in my approach to romance, scaring off suitors with my lack of sophistication? Or was I refreshingly youthful and unafraid to embrace the joys of love without overcomplicating it?

As I contemplated these questions, I realized that there was a delicate balance between self-doubt and self-assurance, between recognizing my worth and acknowledging areas for growth. Instead of dwelling solely on the negative, I used these questions as catalysts for personal development and self-improvement. It was time to find a middle ground, where I could embrace my flaws and insecurities while also celebrating my strengths and unique qualities. This perspective and self-discovery have been guides toward living a more fulfilling and intentional dating life.

With these lessons etched in mind and on my heart, I feel compelled to share a few of my dating experiences. My purpose for sharing is not to shame or blame but rather to offer my experiences as a source of wisdom for other women and to foster an understanding of the highs and lows of dating and the value of the W.A.I.T. Join me on a few remarkable stories of dating, as they are too extraordinary to be left untold.

Some dating situations may be short-lived, but the impact they leave can be lasting. One such experience stands out in my memory. It ensued when he glimpsed me, a stranger at his sister's graduation, and expressed interest in getting to know me. Intrigued, I allowed my friend to share my number with her brother, a man she praised as a great guy. After a few thought-provoking phone conversations, I agreed to go on a blind date. As I arrived at the restaurant, I was pleasantly surprised to see a well-groomed, slim, and handsome man waiting for me. We exchanged greetings with a friendly church hug.

Throughout the evening, we enjoyed each other's company, smiling and engaging in conversation over dinner. As the night progressed, our discussion delved into more personal topics. It became evident that we were both single and casually dating, hoping to find someone interested in a serious, long-term relationship.

Then, without looking up from his plate, he asked me if I had children. Without much thought, I quickly replied, "No." It was at this moment that he raised his head and declared, "Well, I'm glad because I absolutely do not date women with children."

His response was unsettling, and I felt a surge of anger rise within me. I couldn't understand why his statement affected me so deeply.

Collecting myself, I decided to inquire further, asking if he had any children of his own. With a sense of pride, he beamed as he admitted to having three children, two with one mother and one with another.

I was livid. "How does it make sense for you to have children but refuse to date women who have children?" I demanded to know.

"It just makes my life easier," he nonchalantly replied.

Confused, I pressed on, determined to understand his reasoning. "How so?" I asked.

"You know," he said, dismissing my question and attempting to avoid the topic.

I persisted, wanting to hear his explanation. "Easier how?" I probed.

"Well, if you really want to know," he reluctantly admitted, "it takes away the hassle of dating, having to deal with childcare issues and all."

I nodded, though I was inwardly simmering with anger. I desperately wanted to express my frustration, but I sensed there was more foolishness to come.

I continued my line of questioning. "So that's the only reason you date women without children?"

"Well, if I wanted to stay over for the night," he finally countered, "not having kids also makes it easier."

At this point, I had reached my limit. I wanted to flip the table and storm out of the restaurant, but I restrained myself. Another burning question lingered in my mind. I didn't know if I should ask it or if he would even answer. My disgust must have been evident on my face, even though I struggled to maintain a poker face.

I finally gathered the courage to ask him: "What if the mothers of your children wanted to go on a date?"

To my horror, he replied, "They better not leave my children alone to go out with other men."

I was flabbergasted and deeply hurt as a woman. My heart ached for all of the single mothers who had to endure such a mindset from men who had fathered their children. It was disheartening to think that there were men who would refuse to date women with children yet expect the mothers of their own children to prioritize those children over their own personal lives.

Moreover, I felt disheartened for single childless women like me who innocently don't ask the right questions and become unknowingly entangled with such men. It is frustrating to realize that we are being used because our singleness seems most convenient to them until we, too, potentially become baby mother number three. It is a painful reminder of the double standard and lack of consideration that some men exhibit in their dating lives.

At that moment, there was nothing left to say. I realized that I couldn't change his mind set or make him see the error in his thinking. I was willing to take one for the team, for all of the women who have been subjected to such unfair treatment. The date ended without fanfare, and any hopes of a second date or further conversations vanished.

In the months that followed, a walk down memory lane within the pages of my journal would bring me face to face with the reality of my failed dates. These encounters would trigger a flood of emotions and thoughts that would dominate my mind only to remind me of accusations like "you are too picky" or "you are not getting any younger" being hurled at me. At times, I couldn't help but feel a twinge of guilt when relationships did not work out, and I wondered if these men's behavior was just the norm in the world of dating or whether I was indeed "too picky." However, deep down, I knew I couldn't settle for anything less than what I deserved. My loved ones wanted the best for me, and I wanted to find love just as much as they did. Despite the disappointments, I couldn't bring myself to give up on dating as I truly wanted to find that special someone. With that, I made a conscious decision to keep an open heart and continue dating, embracing potential opportunities that came my way.

So, when the most unusual blind date prospect presented itself, I decided to take a chance. It all began when I met a well-groomed older woman at a work conference. We got caught walking side by side as the large crowd filed out of the plenary session. We smiled at each other, an easy conversation ensued, and we ended up sitting at the same table for lunch with six other women.

As we continued chatting, the fact that I was living in Atlanta at the time and was single came up. Without missing a beat, she announced, "Well, isn't that something? My son is single, and he also lives in Atlanta." I couldn't help but notice the mischievous gleam in her eyes. She seemed to be sizing me up, assessing whether I would be a suitable match for her son.

The other women at the table perked up, their curiosity piqued by the possibility of a potential love connection. The matchmaker mama wasted no time in launching into a detailed description of her son's accomplishments and qualities. It was as if she were presenting his résumé to a panel of judges, hoping to secure my interest.

But before she could finish her sales pitch, she abruptly stopped and fixed her gaze on me. With a mix of fascination and hope, she asked, "Would you be open to meeting my son?"

In that moment, all eyes turned toward me, waiting for my response. I felt the weight of their expectations, and I knew I couldn't simply decline.

Caught off guard, I let out a nervous chuckle and replied, "Okay."

The matchmaker mother's face lit up with delight as she exclaimed, "You gotta meet my son!"

It was as if she had won a victory, and the other women at the table couldn't help but share in her excitement. Who would have guessed that my simple lunchtime encounter would end up with me being set up on a blind date?

I gave her my cell phone number, and she told me her son's name and gave me his number. I studied the piece of paper as she handed it to me, telling myself that I would not be the first to call.

As soon as I arrived back in Atlanta, I received a phone call from the son. We spent the evening chatting on the phone, and our conversations continued throughout the following week. They were light and pleasant, filled with laughter and shared interests. So when he finally asked me out for the upcoming weekend, it wasn't hard for me to accept.

As we planned our date, I noticed that he seemed eager to meet up but didn't appear to want to put in too much effort in terms of travel. Technically, he didn't live in Atlanta but on the outskirts, so either way, it would have been a commitment of travel time on both our parts. After some discussion, we decided to meet halfway between our homes.

The day of the date arrived, and I found myself overcome with nervousness. Not only was I anxious about the date itself, but I was also a new driver and not familiar with many places in Atlanta beyond my regular work and home routes. To make matters worse, the traffic was horrendous, and the highway patterns were confusing. Despite my reservations, I didn't want to seem rigid or difficult, so I agreed to make the journey to meet him.

The date itself turned out to be quite pleasant. We had fun exploring the area, trying out a new restaurant, and engaging in deep conversations. I learned a lot about his work in the field of education and sports and his passion for working with at-risk youth. It was refreshing to connect with someone who shared similar values and aspirations.

When the evening ended, I felt a sense of contentment. Despite my initial nerves and uncertainties, the date had gone well, and I was excited to see where this connection could lead. Unbeknownst to me, however, this was a short journey that would test my patience, resilience, and ultimately teach me the importance of listening to my God-given intuition.

He asked for a second date, and I eagerly agreed. This time, he wanted me to venture into his neck of the woods. I was terrified at the thought of driving that distance, but he seemed inflexible with his suggestion. Against my better judgment, I agreed to go without expressing my uneasiness.

I got the address and drove to his home. When I arrived, we got into his car and drove to an arcade for some fun. We played games, shot pool, and even had a few rounds of bowling. It was a lighthearted and enjoyable evening. My childlike side emerged, and we laughed and bonded over the games.

When the evening began to wind down, I started to feel a sense of anxiety. The realization hit me that I would have to navigate my way back home in the cover of night. I mentioned my uneasiness to him, but he didn't seem to care. He didn't offer to guide me or even suggest following him to the entrance of the highway. We rode back to his home to retrieve my car, and the silence in the car was deafening as I worried about how I would make it home.

I hurried to my car, refusing his advances for a kiss or a goodnight embrace. He looked incredulous, but I didn't let it faze me. I nervously fumbled with my keys, eventually managing to put them in the ignition. Judging from my drive time there, I embarked on what should have been a forty-minute drive back home. Instead, the journey turned out to be a terrifying and seemingly never-ending adventure that took almost three hours.

As I started the drive, I realized that I had directions to my destination but not for the return. Panic set in as I drove around in circles for what felt like hours. I prayed and asked God for guidance, but instead I encountered a few showers of blessings. I didn't have GPS, and I was too afraid to stop and ask for directions. The surrounding area were isolated, and the few lighted spots seemed sketchy. I kept my eyes on the gas gauge, fearing that I would run out of fuel. Overwhelmed, I felt tears streaming down my face and blurring my vision.

Desperately, I looked for a sign that said I-285, a major highway that encircles Atlanta. I knew that if I saw that sign, I would have a surefire way of finding the road home. At long last, I began recognizing fast-food joints and well-lit gas stations. The signs that alerted travelers of their distance from key landmarks started to look familiar. Joy washed over me when I saw the on-ramp sign for I-285. I can't recall which direction I went, but knowing it was a circle and would bring me to my desired exit comforted me. I felt relieved that I was finally seeing the light at the end of the tunnel.

I drove the circle for a short distance before my designated exit appeared. There it was—exit 31B in full view! And with that, I knew home was just minutes away. I pulled up to my apartment complex, pressed the opener that hung on my visor, and anxiously waited. I watched as the imposing iron gate, untouched by my recent ordeal, slowly, almost gracefully, slid open and beckoned me home. I entered and parked in my designated spot in the garage and let out the biggest sigh of relief. I thanked God for bringing me home safely. I was extremely tired but happy to have made it.

I didn't feel like calling my date to announce my safe arrival home as he hadn't checked in with me even with the three-hour passage of time. Nonetheless, I decided to give him a courtesy call, but my outreach never progressed beyond his phone just ringing in my ear. He never returned my call, neither did he call the next day to see if I had made it home safely.

I couldn't help but hope for a follow-up message, a simple gesture to show that he cared. But the days turned into weeks, and the weeks turned into months, and it became very clear that he had no intention of reaching out again. The silence spoke volumes, leaving me with a lingering sense of disappointment.

Points to Ponder

- We all can relate to the thrill and the initial excitement of meeting someone new, particularly in the context of a blind date, and the range of emotions and thoughts it can evoke. The key is to manage expectations and stay open to different outcomes—a skill that can be cultivated over time.

- Remember that dating is a process of gathering information and getting to know someone. It is important to ask questions and have meaningful conversations to learn more about each other. Approach dates with a sense of fun and openness, without being too attached to any specific outcome. Avoid allowing eagerness and the thrill of meeting someone new to cloud your judgment or leave you feeling disappointed or vulnerable. Stay true to yourself and your own boundaries, and trust that the right connection will come in due time.

WHAT OTHER SINGLE WOMEN ARE SAYING

Is faith or spirituality important in your life? How does that impact your dating/waiting decisions?

- "I want to be equally yoked with someone or, at least, on the same spiritual path. Without this, I don't believe a relationship will be as meaningful for me."

- "I find it hard to connect intimately with men who have no faith foundation or who are not practicing Christians."

- "I would like for my partner to also be spiritual and make decisions, lead life based on those principles that we both share."

—Single Woman Survey respondents

Chapter Nine
I THOUGHT HE WAS THE ONE

Above all else, guard your heart, for everything you do flows from it.
PROVERBS 4:23

It was a blind date; he was a friend of a friend. It was the only blind date that left me smitten and blindsided—not once but twice. He had me hook, line, and sinker. I was in love! For the first time in my adult life, I felt like I was in a grown-up relationship. Our courtship was fun, respectful, and consistent. He checked in regularly and kept his word, we had the best soulful conversations, and most important, he loved the Lord. Can I get a hallelujah?

During our courtship, I was exposed to the finer things in life, and I was shown a side of the city I called home that I had no idea existed or that I thought was reserved for the elites. We frequented the theaters—a world that was all new to me—and we dined at the finest restaurants. I got most excited by his culinary skills and the mix of mouthwatering dishes he would serve up when he cooked at his home. After six months of dating, I found myself in a state of bliss. Little did I know, a storm was brewing on the horizon.

One fateful night, as I lay in a deep sleep, the jarring ring of the landline telephone jolted me awake. Confused and disoriented, I stumbled toward the phone, my heart pounding in my chest. It was him, my love interest, on the other end of the line. His voice quivered with urgency as he declared that he wanted to get married and that he wanted it to happen soon.

My mind raced with a mix of excitement and confusion. Was this the moment I had been waiting for? Was he about to propose? But before I could even process my thoughts, he uttered four words that crushed my dreams: "but not to you."

Time seemed to stand still as his words echoed in my ears. I felt as if I were floating, having an out-of-body experience. How could this be happening? Just moments ago, we were living a fairy-tale romance, and now it was all collapsing around me.

He continued to speak, showering me with compliments and justifications for his decision. He claimed that we hadn't known each other long enough and said that he was in a hurry to settle down, get married, and have a family. I felt a whirlwind of emotions as I struggled to make sense of the nonsense I was hearing. Hadn't we shared deep conversations and built a strong connection? Hadn't he seen a future with me?

Heartbroken and bewildered, I listened as he revealed his plan to rekindle his relationship with an ex-girlfriend. It was a devastating blow, as I realized that I had been nothing more than a temporary distraction.

In the months that followed, I watched from a distance as he swiftly moved on, marrying an ex-girlfriend, and picking up where they had supposedly left off. It was a bitter pill to swallow, knowing that I had been replaced so easily. But through the pain, I found solace in the knowledge that I deserved someone who would choose me wholeheartedly, without hesitation or doubt.

Fast forward about seven years to a snowy Good Friday morning, when I received an unexpected call from him. It was a jumble of apologies for the heartless way he had ended our dating relationship years earlier. I listened politely, unsure of how to react to this sudden flood of information. I can't recall exactly what I said in response, but I remember holding the phone away from my ear, staring at it in confusion. The conversation felt random and out of place.

Despite the pain of our past, I had moved on with my life, focusing on my career and personal growth. After that Good Friday call, I thought I would never hear from him again. But to my surprise, several years later, he reappeared in my life. This time he revealed that his marriage had crumbled and that he was on the brink of divorce. This was the same marriage he had rushed into because he wanted to settle down and have a family, the marriage for which he had decided I was not "the one." The demise of his marriage had left him feeling lost and alone. As he made his way through the divorce process, I went against my better judgment and became his empathetic listener, a familiar friend. I allowed myself to be his sounding board, getting pulled into the chaos and madness of his divorce proceedings. I found myself eagerly awaiting his relentless phone calls, even though I knew doing so wasn't healthy for me.

By this time in our lives, we lived in different states, but we found ways to connect. During our long commutes, we took advantage of the time by having extensive secret phone conversations. It became a routine for us to spend hours talking, sometimes up to two or three hours a day. We would discuss a wide range of topics, using this time to connect and stay close despite the physical distance between us.

In addition to our commute conversations, we found other

moments throughout the day to continue our discussions. Whether it was while he ran errands, walked his dog, or went to the gym, he made sure to find time for "safe" phone conversations, meaning that they were out of the earshot of anyone who would find such dialogue suspicious or even highly inappropriate considering his tumultuous marital status.

The frequency of our phone calls was so high that my phone constantly rang. To this day, I keep my phone on silent as the constant ringing during that time has left a lasting impact, likely related to the stress and emotional toll of that period in my life.

Eventually, our conversations shifted from the challenges of his divorce proceedings to discussions about what life could be like after his divorce. He consistently expressed his belief that single life was not for him and that he wanted to marry me. Like clockwork, my mind fell into a pattern known as "rosy retrospection," where I began to view our past relationship through rose-colored glasses, remembering it in a more favorable light. Memories of our incredible dating experience years ago flooded back, and I found myself yearning to relive those feelings once again. I convinced myself that it was possible that I had fallen for this man all over again. It felt justified to me—after all, we knew each other, we had a history, and we shared a deep love and respect for each other. We both had a strong faith in the Lord, and we even had mutual friends. It seemed like half the battle was already won.

Emotionally entangled and vulnerable, I found myself creating spaces within my mind and heart to hold his pain. The respect I had for this man was unparalleled. It was a feeling that came naturally, without pretense or manipulation. This degree of bonding with another human being was new to me. The authenticity and reality of these emotions were undeniable, making them challenging to ignore or dismiss. However, despite the soulfulness of our connection, on those rare occasions when we would see each other in person, I made the conscious decision to draw the line at full physical intimacy. I believed that not engaging in sexual intercourse somehow made kissing, heavy petting, and sensual conversations harmless indiscretions. This was the lie I repeatedly told myself, but it was far from the truth.

The truth is that these small acts of intimacy, even without sexual intercourse, created a deep emotional connection and strengthened our bond. I was naive to believe that I could separate the physical and emotional aspects of our relationship. As time passed, I remained oblivious to the reality of my situation, unknowingly entangling myself in a web of emotions while nurturing a lie.

Countless hours were wasted on phone calls, with me consoling his irrational fears and holding back my tears. During those moments, I often daydreamed about what life would be like once this nightmare of an ordeal was over. Then finally, the day arrived—the day he would be divorced and once again be a "free" man. We spoke the evening before as we always did. I wished him well, and in that moment, I sensed our shared unspoken desire for this chapter to be behind us.

On his divorce proceedings day, I was traveling for work and decided to have lunch alone in the hotel restaurant, fully expecting to receive his call. But to my dismay, there was nothing but silence. The much-anticipated phone call never came. I frantically checked my phone, making sure it was charged and the ringer was on. Everything seemed to be in order, yet there were no missed calls, no texts—nothing.

The entire day passed by without a single word from him. This was highly unusual considering our past interactions. He was always the one to initiate contact, so for the first time in what felt like forever, I mustered up the courage to call him. Holding my breath, I dialed his number, unsure of what I would hear on the other end. My emotions were running wild.

To my immense relief, he finally answered the phone after what felt like an eternity on what must have been the twelfth ring. I silently exhaled, gathering my strength. I asked him how he was doing and how things had gone. I waited anxiously for his response, even attempting to predict what he might say. But the five words that echoed through the phone shattered my expectations: "you need to ask God." Confused and taken aback, I stammered, "Wait! What? Who? Why?"

As a Christian who believes God's ability to work wonders, I thought at first that the final divorce hearing had gone miraculously well. However, that was not what he was implying. After uttering those five words, he abruptly hung up the phone, leaving me in a state of shock and confusion. From that moment on, all forms of communication ceased. The once constant flow of conversation, which had felt like a full-time job, was replaced with complete silence. My phone stopped ringing, and the silence became deafening. I felt conflicted, alone, and desperate to be heard, but there was no one to listen. To cope, I turned off the ringer, shutting out the world.

The following weeks were the most difficult I have ever experienced. My heart physically ached, as if it had been shattered into a million pieces. The pain was tangible, and it felt as though I had lost a dear friend. My dreams and plans were shattered, and I was left to pick up the pieces. I began dissecting every moment of our relationship, searching for signs and clues that may have led to its demise. I longed for closure, but instead, I was left with a deep sense of sadness and shame.

The passage of time had brought a glimmer of hope, a sense that the wounds of the past were slowly healing. I had started to believe that I was on the path to recovery, that the pain would eventually fade away. But life has a way of throwing unexpected curveballs, and just when I thought I was moving forward, the scabs were abruptly ripped off, exposing the raw, tender flesh beneath. It felt as if someone had taken a knife and sliced open my heart, leaving me vulnerable and exposed to the world.

The shock and disbelief washed over me like a tidal wave as I learned the news. Less than a year later, he had remarried. The realization hit me with a force I couldn't comprehend. How could he move on so quickly? How could he replace me so easily? The questions swirled in my mind, each one a dagger to my already wounded heart. I cried out to God, desperate for answers, for some semblance of understanding. But the silence was deafening, and the answers never came.

As the tears streamed down my face, I couldn't help but feel a mix of emotions. Anger, betrayal, and a deep sense of loss consumed me. I had given so much of myself to this person, only to be discarded and replaced. It felt like a cruel twist of fate, a final blow to my already shattered heart.

In that moment, all I could do was weep. As I wept, I hoped and prayed that my night of weeping would bring joy in the morning, but it seemed that joy would never come. The pain was too much to bear, the weight of it crushing my spirit. I questioned if healing was truly possible, if time could ever mend the wounds that seemed to grow deeper with each passing day. The tears flowed freely, a release of the pent-up emotions that had been building inside me. And as I wept, I prayed to God for strength and for the courage to pick up the pieces and find a way to heal, even in the face of such heartbreak.

With a renewed sense of self-worth and a commitment to prioritize my own happiness, I began to rebuild my life. I surrounded myself with supportive friends and family who reminded me of my strength and resilience. I focused on my own personal growth, pursuing hobbies and interests that brought me joy and fulfillment.

As time passed, the pain of rejection slowly faded, replaced by a newfound sense of empowerment. I realized that I deserved someone who would love and cherish me, someone who would be committed and faithful. I vowed never to settle for anything less.

I took the lessons learned from this experience and applied them to my future relationships. I became more intentional in my dating life, carefully choosing partners who aligned with my values and treated me with the respect and love I deserved. I set clear boundaries and communicated my needs and expectations openly and honestly.

In the end, this heartbreak served as a lesson for personal growth and self-discovery. It taught me the importance of self-love and the power of letting go. I emerged from the pain stronger and more resilient, ready to embrace the love and happiness that awaited me in the future.

Points to Ponder

- Being hurt, heartbroken, or dumped by someone you really loved is devastating, but it's the risk you take when you step into the arena of love and relationship with another person.
- Remember that healing takes time. It is essential to be patient and compassionate with yourself. Surround yourself with a support system of friends and family who can provide love and encouragement. Take time for self-care by engaging in an activity that helps you connect with yourself, process your emotions, and gain clarity on your thoughts and feelings.

WHAT OTHER SINGLE WOMEN ARE SAYING

Do you have a list (written or in your head) of the characteristics of your ideal mate? Has this list changed over time? If your answer is yes, please mention how it has changed over time.

- "It has become more about how the person treats me, values me, and expresses his love toward me versus some of the superficial things I used to value."

- "Physical characteristics aren't as important as much as they were before. They are important, just not high priority. Spirituality has the highest priority. He must be able to pray. The husband, for me, must earn equal to my income, if not more than what I have."

—Single Woman Survey respondents

WHAT MARRIED OR FORMERLY MARRIED WOMEN ARE SAYING

- "Get to know yourself first. Respect yourself. Get to know your partner. Don't rush anything. Through communication and actions, you would be able to figure out if your partner is compatible."

- "Be clear and unapologetic about your values and standards. Pay close attention to what your partner says. Believe the self they present to you. Don't think you can change them."

—Married Woman Survey respondents

Chapter Ten
VALUES AND BOUNDARIES

Do not conform to the pattern of this world, but be transformed by the renewing of your mind. Then you will be able to test and approve what God's will is—his good, pleasing and perfect will.

ROMANS 12:2

I can relate to the struggle of losing sight of one's values and identity as a woman in the dating world. It is easy to enter a relationship with confidence, believing that I know exactly who I am. But then, unexpectedly, I find myself faced with a situation that forces me to choose between my prince and my principles. In those moments, my instincts scream at me to make a different choice, to stand up for myself, or to leave. However, I often ignore my intuition, stay silent, and overstay my welcome.

Days later, as I gather my senses and regain my dignity, I am filled with horror and disbelief as I look at myself in the mirror. I try to reconcile what just happened and how easy it was to live a hijacked life—but it is often too late. Whether I have compromised my values to appease someone or tolerated repeated deception, I have found myself in those situations more times than I care to admit. In those moments of self-betrayal, I have made a promise to myself and to God that I will never allow any man to treat me that way again. However, to my disbelief, I have found myself repeating the same old patterns.

In those instances when I didn't feel like an equal in a relationship or when I was disrespected, I realized that it was because I had willingly handed over all my power or failed to use my voice. Despite knowing deep down that something was off, I still allowed myself to engage in those situations. I am in no way condoning such insults, but it wasn't solely the other person's fault; I also had a role to play in what happened. I could have chosen to walk away and protect myself and my sanity, but instead I chose to stay and endure the nonsense. Upon reflection, I realized that I needed to take responsibility for my own actions and choices.

Over the years, whenever a relationship ended, I would find myself in a state of introspection, analyzing every detail and trying to understand where things went wrong. Hoping to gain some clarity, I would even go as far as asking suitors for their perspective on the demise of our relationship. However, apart from them thinking I had lost it, their responses often fell short of satisfying my curiosity and didn't provide the closure I was seeking.

After realizing the pointlessness of my quest and the negative impact it had on my confidence, I decided to take a different approach to dating. Looking for clear answers, I embarked on a deeper exploration of biblical guidance on relationships. To my surprise, I discovered that the Bible does not explicitly address the concept of dating as we understand it today; and for a minute, I was left wondering if dating was indeed a biblical concept.

However, as I studied the Bible, I discovered a wealth of valuable principles and instructions that resonated with me and that could be applied to relationships between men and women, including those in the context of dating. These principles include maintaining sexual integrity, seeking God's guidance in relationships, connecting with those who share similar faith and values, and fostering a mutual level of respect and selflessness.

I expanded my understanding of relationships and dating by actively seeking wisdom, advice, and guidance from trusted friends and mentors. I wasn't shy about reaching out to them for their insights and experiences because they were the people I thought of as members of my trusted circle. Additionally, I journaled a lot and immersed myself in books, sermons, podcasts, and workshops that focused on relationships and dating.

Through my study, I stumbled onto Gary Chapman's book *The Five Love Languages*. Though it is written for couples, I dug into it with insatiable eagerness, and it became a game changer for me. The premise of the book is that understanding and speaking your partner's primary love language is essential for a fulfilling and lasting relationship. I found that these principles were applicable in fostering general friendship and in dating.

I also found that attending singles ministries, workshops, and seminars provided valuable opportunities to learn from experts and engage in discussions with others who were also seeking growth in this area. Finally, I utilized the Internet as a resource, exploring many websites and even enrolling in a private virtual membership program that offered personal and group coaching, information, and perspectives on relationships.

I have reached a point in my life where I feel completely at ease expressing my values as a woman. It was a journey that required time and introspection as I sought answers to a series of challenging questions, I developed from various sources throughout my learning process. The core questions included:

- What are the principles that I firmly believe in and that I will never compromise on?
- What qualities do I genuinely admire in others?
- What kind of person do I desire to be?
- What brings me real joy?
- What aspects of my life do I prioritize?

Answering these questions required deep soul-searching as I aimed to be honest and thoughtful in my responses. Through this process, I had the courage to identify and embrace faith, respect, honesty, health, generosity, gratitude, and wisdom as the core values that resonate with me on a profound level.

During this time of personal reflection as I delved into the process of refining my values, I gained a newfound clarity regarding the importance of setting boundaries. It became evident that my values and boundaries are deeply intertwined, and one was the foundation on which the other stood.

There were boundaries that I immediately knew had to be established and affirmed. They were as basic as requesting a courtesy phone call rather than having someone show up unannounced at my home and as courageous as letting suitors know that I am on an abstinence journey and that I will not engage in sexual activity while dating. This was a giant step because in the past I had not been particularly good at establishing, stating, and maintaining boundaries in my dating relationships. It felt as though my boundaries were equivalent to drawing a line in the sand, only for them to gradually be washed away by the incoming tide. These tides were the small offenses that occurred over time, slowly eroding trust and stifling all hopes and desires for what the relationship could be.

Making the decision at the age of forty-two to abstain from sex was more challenging to explain than to put into practice. Despite never allowing myself to be driven by sex or making it the focal point of my relationships and instead taking the time to truly get to know the person I was dating, this approach often proved to be difficult to implement. It became clear that no amount of gathering information, vetting someone's character, or following the ninety-day rule could guarantee success. The ninety-day rule comes from the book *Act Like a Lady, Think Like a Man*. According to author Steve Harvey, the ninety-day rule is the minimum amount of time that a woman should wait before becoming sexually intimate with a man. Harvey feels that this time gives both people the opportunity to get to know each other on a deeper level. Furthermore, it allows the woman to gauge the man's intention and possible commitment beyond the physical. These were solid instructions; however, it was not until I really assessed my own core values and beliefs that I was led to abandon my vague boundaries and establish a wall of sexual purity in my dating life.

Despite unwavering support from some people in my life, my decision was also met by others with skepticism and sarcasm. But I remained determined. Men and women alike would often respond with comments like "good luck," implying that it was nearly impossible to achieve such self-control. Some would snap back with comments like "better you than me" or "I would just die," insinuating that I possessed a unique willpower that other women or men lacked. Others would cautiously ask "so what would you do when…," their voice trailing off as they struggled to find the right words. I would meet their gaze and inquire, "when what?" This forced them to confront their assumptions. They would then timidly ask, with a hint of a smirk, how I would handle sexual desires, as if they were a disease and that sex was the only cure. With a straight face, I would add a touch of humor, letting them know that I would simply take a cold shower and pray.

Seven years later, at the ripe old age of forty-nine, I guess cold showers and prayer were no match for my fleshly desire when I found myself in a compromised place. I had broken my vow of abstinence and had had sex. On one hand, there was a sense of satisfaction and a renewed feeling of connection and intimacy with a potential partner; we had known each other for almost two years, and it felt like there was a possibility of a relationship. On the other hand, I couldn't shake the feelings of guilt, regret, and disappointment. I constantly questioned whether I had made the right decision and felt overwhelmed with guilt for abandoning my values and beliefs.

The internal conflict of breaking my commitment to abstinence weighed heavily on me, and I struggled for a long time to reconcile my actions with my personal convictions. For weeks, I found myself feeling vulnerable and anxious, my mind consumed with self-doubt, worry, and even a fear of judgment from others. It became clear that I needed to put a stop to this self-inflicted torture. I couldn't continue dragging myself through the abstinence hall of shame as if my life were over.

I made the decision to have a hard and honest chat with myself, acknowledging that I needed to seek counsel from someone who would not judge me or pry for unnecessary details. So I reached out to a therapist whom I had spoken to before on other issues related to a career shift. I believed that having a thoughtful conversation with a trusted confidant would help me process my emotions and navigate the internal conflicts and personal concerns I was facing.

Leading up to the encounter, I had communicated with my partner several times that I was on an abstinence journey. But I admit that my communication was not as assertive as it should have been. Additionally, I made the careless decision to place myself in an environment that did not support my goal, and I take full responsibility for that.

The most important lesson I have learned on my journey of abstinence is the importance of doing it for the right reasons. Abstinence should not be seen as a badge of honor used to boast about the number of years one has abstained, as that holds little significance for most individuals, especially men. Instead, it is crucial to embark on and maintain an abstinent lifestyle for the right motives. Personally, I have come to realize that my abstinence is deeply connected to my relationship with God and His desires for me as a human being. It aligns with what His word teaches about sexual purity. Once this understanding dawned on me, I no longer viewed my abstinence journey in terms of its duration. It has become a way of life, something I embrace because I am a child of the divine and because it is what He expects from me.

I have since moved on from that person and that experience, and I no longer feel guilty about it. I recognize that as a human being, I am prone to making mistakes even in situations where my intentions are good. The most important thing I can do for myself now is to show myself compassion and forgiveness and to reflect on the lessons that can be learned from this experience.

Points to Ponder

- Identifying and defining your core values may seem overwhelming, but it is a worthwhile endeavor if you dedicate the necessary time to develop them.

- Remember that values can change over time as you have new experiences and evolve as a person. Your values are a good foundation for creating boundaries. Don't view your boundaries as invisible walls that you use to protect yourself from men but rather a valuable tool for fostering respect and security. Without clearly stated boundaries, your suitor may not know what is acceptable or when he has crossed a line. With boundaries, co-dependency is less likely: boundaries allow each person in the relationship to maintain their own unique identity.

WHAT OTHER SINGLE WOMEN ARE SAYING

What do you bring to the table?

- "I *am* the table; Mr. Right needs to pull up and hope he matches the decor."

- "Any man involved with me would get a well-rounded package—intelligence, good looks, fun, great domestic skills, trustworthiness, spiritually evolved, financially sound. In total, a great partner."

- "I don't answer it. I've never been asked it, and I wouldn't answer it. My value as a person, woman, and life partner is obvious for a man who knows himself, is emotionally healthy, and has a vision for his life."

—*Single Woman Survey respondents*

Chapter Eleven
WHAT DO YOU BRING TO THE TABLE?

> A wife of noble character who can find? She is worth far more than rubies. Her husband has full confidence in her and lacks nothing of value. She brings him good, not harm, all the days of her life.
>
> PROVERBS 31:10-12

The frequently asked question "What do you bring to the table?" has always struck me as interesting. What stands out to me is that it seems to be a rhetorical question and that it is often asked by men of women in terms of what they can contribute to the relationship, especially when they might be entertaining thought of marriage. Even when men ask this question with apparent conviction, it seems like they don't really care about receiving an answer. Over time, it has become a common phrase that is repeated in conversations, much like the saying that "relationships need to be fifty-fifty." But what does the idea of what you bring to the table really mean in the context of a committed love relationship and marriage?

Imagine my surprise when my younger sister, Kim, who had been married for almost two decades, asked me this exact question. It was during the Christmas holidays, and we were both in her kitchen making breakfast when she suddenly said, "Let's talk." The tone in her voice indicated that she had been pondering something for a while and had finally found the right moment to bring it up. Normally, I am the one initiating these types of conversations that make her and the rest of our family flee in fear of my line of questioning. So I was thrilled and eagerly awaited what she had to say.

As she continued to whip the pancake batter, she unexpectedly posed the question, "So, sis, you want to get married. Let's talk about what you bring to the table."

I was taken aback by her inquiry. I, a woman known for her chattiness, was rendered speechless. Personally, I had never been directly asked this question by a man, and I struggled to find the right words to respond. In that moment, I wished I had my journal to jot down my thoughts and work through them.

However, before I could gain my bearings, she repeated the question, sensing my hesitation and lack of words. Her expectant stare intensified the pressure, forcing me to gather my thoughts and list the attributes I believed I brought to the table.

Then with a sense of excitement, I started to recite my offerings.

"Well," I began, "I have a stable job, and I own my own home."

My sister silently waited for more.

Gazing at the ceiling as if the answer were written there, I continued.

"I have a nice car, I have two degrees, I am a skilled cook, and I can maintain a clean and organized home."

At this point, I was in the flow, enthusiastically listing what I brought to the metaphorical table. I barely paused as I rattled off my qualities.

Then I became aware of my sister's silence. I looked at her to see if I could tell what she was thinking.

With her head tilted to one side and her brows slightly raised, she looked at me utterly bewildered as if I had lost my mind.

"What?" I asked.

I tried to comprehend how I could have gone astray with what I had just shared. "After all," I thought to myself, "shouldn't my domestic abilities and educational achievements account for something?"

Then without warning, my thought was interrupted.

"No, no, no," she said, looking straight into my eyes. "Those are nice things to have, and I don't discount them, but those are not what you bring to the table for marriage."

She paused for a moment, then forged ahead to the crux of the matter.

"Everything on your list could be paid for by a man," she said. "A man could hire someone to clean his house, cook his food, and even do his laundry."

I listened intently and found myself nodding in agreement, as what she had just said was starting to make sense.

"A man could even pay for sex!" she exclaimed.

I suddenly perked up. All of my senses were on alert, not because of what I just heard but because of the jolting effect of her final statement. I wanted to laugh, but the seriousness of the conversation weighed on me.

My sister continued to share her insights. "When was the last time a man assessed your educational accomplishments or culinary skills prior to asking you out on a date?"

My mind drew a blank as I tried to recall any such instance. I let out a tiny chuckle as I admitted that it had never happened. Then both of us giggled, feeling like two high school girls amused by the sheer ridiculousness of that line of questioning as a possible pick-up line.

I was captivated by the conversation, and I wanted to explore its depths. It felt like a juicy mix of wisdom and wit, and I savored every moment, absorbing all of the insight and knowledge being shared.

I took a breath as I recovered from the laughter we had just shared and then delved deeper.

"What are men really looking for women to bring to the table?" I asked my sister.

As if she had rehearsed this list countless times, my sister began reciting her own version of qualities that men are seeking in marriage.

"Well," she said, "men generally look for soft qualities in women, such as emotional support, shared interests, effective communication skills, a calm and peaceful presence, problem-solving abilities, alignment in values and beliefs, and sexual compatibility, just to name a few."

I remained quiet. I didn't feel the need to agree or deny, so I just listened. The concepts were not new to me, but the context intrigued me, and despite a bit of uneasiness surrounding a few of the qualities men desired, I yearned to learn more.

But first I needed to reconcile in my mind that what I had just heard was not written in stone. I understood that in relationships, it takes two to make it work. I then expressed to her my feeling that the qualities I had just heard her list were qualities that I, too, desired and deserved in a mate.

This exchange was a gift that proved to be instructive, as I genuinely acquired new knowledge that Christmas morning. I walked away from that conversation with mixed feelings. I had always hung on to my educational and professional attainments coupled with my domestic abilities as valuable assets in marriage. But now I began wondering if I had been misguided. I realized that there must be two sides to this story and that I needed to know what men brought to the table as well. I began reflecting on my infamous list, which I had written out so many times over the years. It had evolved from the superficial qualities like tall, dark, and handsome as a dizzy teenage girl to more substantial, abiding, and fundamental traits like trustworthiness, emotional intelligence, compatibility, and shared values as an adult.

After that conversation with my sister, I became intrigued and decided to delve deeper into the topic. I started reading and researching, exploring different perspectives, and observing conversations on social media. It was clear that there were varying opinions on the matter. Some people believed in being upfront and asking what a partner brings to the table, while others strongly opposed the question altogether. As I researched further, I came across some people who vehemently disagree with asking the question. These people argue that instead of asking this question, both individuals in a dating relationship should observe each other's words and actions over time to see if their desirable qualities and values align. They believe that actions speak louder than words when it comes to truly understanding someone.

Then I had a brilliant idea. I realized that it would be valuable to gather insights from other women who, like me, may not have been actively engaged in the social media conversations and debates surrounding this topic. These were single women over thirty-five who expressed a desire to be married. I decided to conduct a survey, posing several questions related to life as a single person and the dating experience. (I also later surveyed married women, as I wanted to get their perspective on these issues, too.) One specific question I asked the single women was how they would answer the question, "What do you bring to the table?" To my surprise, the women were incredibly vocal and had a wealth of perspectives to share on the subject. The responses fell in both camps—those who thought the question should be asked and those who thought it shouldn't be posed. One woman even declared, "I *am* the table!"

Personally, I can see the value in both sides of the debate. I enjoy engaging in deep conversations and hearing how a person thinks and articulates his ideas, so I would likely ask some version of the question "what do you bring to the table?" However, I also recognize the importance of observing a person's behavior over time to gauge his interest and compatibility. Ultimately, for me, it's a combination of both asking and observing that can provide a more comprehensive understanding of a potential partner.

Points to Ponder

- What is your reaction to the question "what do you bring to the table"? Do you think it's a fair question to be asked by a man who seeks to know the qualities of a potential wife?
- Remember that the question of what you bring to the table does not have a one-size-fits-all answer. It requires self-reflection, open communication, and a willingness to understand and appreciate the qualities and strengths of both you and your potential partner. By discussing this question or by observing, you can foster a strong and harmonious relationship built on mutual respect and understanding.

WHAT OTHER SINGLE WOMEN ARE SAYING

Share your experiences/feelings on the dating or waiting journey.

- "At fifty-two, I am finding it challenging finding someone compatible. When I do, they are not that interested because they want someone younger. Being in Houston, a lot of the men in this age group are retired, and I am busy with running my business."

- "The dating scene is tough as I get older. The dating apps are not helpful and lack authenticity. People look at superficial things such as ethnicity, job, location, as well as other requirements."

—Single Woman Survey respondents

Chapter Twelve
MENOPAUSE DARED ME TO DUMP DATING

> Be pleased to save me, Lord; come quickly, Lord, to help me.
>
> PSALMS 40:13

Menopause is a natural cycle in a woman's life that often brings unexpected changes and challenges. It courses through in phases, the first being perimenopause, which can sometimes be so subtle that it goes unnoticed by many busy women. I was told that it would happen within a certain age range, perhaps between fifty-one and fifty-five, but that it can take place as early as forty-five. With such an arbitrary time of arrival, I was not going to just sit around or put my life on hold waiting for menopause to show up.

At first, her entrance into my life was very subtle—she was like a well-behaved guest. I like to think that she was silently scouting out her surroundings in anticipation of the havoc she was about to wreak on my life. It soon became clear that this visitor had no intention of leaving. I either needed to adapt to life with this intruder or live in perpetual denial of her existence. It wasn't long before I found out the latter was impossible to do. Coupled with dating, menopause was a royal nightmare for me.

I was fifty-one years old when it all started. One of the first signs I was beginning my menopausal journey was the irregularity of my menstrual cycle. Sometimes my period would disappear altogether, leaving me confused and not sure on how make mundane decisions like "should I wear those white pants?" or "can I risk it and go to the beach today?" Other times, it would arrive unexpectedly, catching me off guard while I was in public, causing embarrassment, discomfort, and inconvenience. Then there were days when my period was so heavy that no manner of sanitary products was a match for this crimson flood. In times like these, all I could do was sit it out and wait for this silent storm to pass.

Then I noticed a significant decline in my tolerance level, causing even the smallest events or actions to trigger intense reactions. It became evident that I was in trouble and needed to address my mood when I found myself one day impulsively following a driver who had cut me off in traffic. Normally, such an incident wouldn't have bothered me, but on this day, I was consumed with anger and a strong desire to teach him a lesson. I trailed this stranger until he reached his destination, which ended up being a veterinary clinic parking lot. As he stepped out of his car and entered the clinic, I suddenly snapped back to reality. To my surprise, he was a police officer driving an unmarked vehicle. Overwhelmed with fear, regret, and shame, I turned off my ignition, slumped over my steering wheel, and began sobbing uncontrollably. As I regained clarity, I began questioning my actions and asking myself, "What on earth was that, and what is wrong with you, Vanessa?" I was shaken and mortified—it felt as if I had had an out-of-body experience. It was at that moment that I made a firm decision to consistently monitor my mood and actively engage in practices such as deep breathing and stillness. But most important, I prayed a lot about this issue, as I knew I couldn't humanly manage the anger and poor tolerance level that accompanied these symptoms.

One of the most frustrating symptoms was the internal thermostat that seemed to be constantly tinkered with. I would experience these bouts of internal warmness as if I were consuming a warm beverage followed by being enveloped in a cozy blanket. Then out of the blue, there would be intense heat waves, also known as hot flashes. They would cruelly surge through my body without warning or concern as to my whereabouts. The sheer distress of the episode made me want to strip off all my clothes and immerse my body in cold water. It was maddening. This made dating extremely difficult as I couldn't maintain an ounce of composure under these circumstances of near combustion.

I remember a particular moment from a lovely first date. Everything was going well as I enjoyed the atmosphere, the music, the food, and the company of my new suitor. I was sipping on a virgin piña colada, one of my go-to cocktails that satisfied both my aversion to alcohol and my attempt to cool the internal volcano. Then without warning, I felt the heat rising from within. I considered excusing myself from the table, but instead I quickly rummaged through my purse for my black, handheld, battery-operated mini-fan and a wad of paper towel. I braced myself for the inevitable.

When I looked up, my date was smiling at me, appearing relaxed and happy for a split second. But before this thought fully left my mind, his smile began to fade, replaced by a look of concern washing over his face.

"Are you okay?" he asked, reaching over to gently pat my arm.

"Yes," I replied, trying to discreetly tap my face to rid myself of the beads of sweat that were popping off my face.

"You don't look good," he said, sounding even more concerned.

Before I could respond, he handed me my water and suggested, "Drink some. It might help."

My mini-fan at full throttle and my attempts to mop up my face were no match for the moment. The heat radiated up my spine, and I could feel the river of sweat as it slid down my back.

My date grabbed the laminated menu and began fanning me like a lunatic, still asking if I was okay.

"But you're drenched!" he exclaimed, observing the sweat dripping from under my chin onto my neck, cascading down my chest, then disappearing into the seam of my V-necked blouse.

"Do you feel like you're going to faint or something?" he asked, his tone filled with worry.

"Should we call 911?" he added, attempting to catch the waitress's attention.

"No!" I shouted through clenched teeth. "I'm just fine."

"But...," he started, staring at me, my fan, and my soaking wet paper towel, trying to make sense of what he had just witnessed.

The hot flash disappeared as quickly as it had come, leaving me sapped of my energy and baffled about the stark differences of the before and after.

I tried to explain to my date what had just happened, but he only seemed more perplexed. I attributed his confusion to our eleven-year age difference and his ignorance about the journey of a mature woman.

This date was just one of many embarrassing episodes I experienced. I found myself in a constant state of discomfort due to the regular occurrence of my hot flashes and their accompanying symptoms. The hot flashes became a hindrance to my personal and professional life, daring me to dump entirely the thought of dating. Each day, I prayed for this misery to taper off or disappear altogether as a way to reclaim my life and find some relief. I couldn't fathom accepting this as a permanent way of life. Even ten years would be way too long.

It was disheartening to hear other women talk about their own experiences with menopause, some having endured it for a decade or more. Basically, the daily hot flashes, night sweats, and mood swings lasted well into their seventies. I was mortified just listening to some of these stories and couldn't help but feel discouraged. I dreaded my future at the thought of menopause and its life-sucking craziness being part of my journey. Then there was a silent resentment that brewed within me toward women who flaunted the fact that they had sailed through this phase of life. Except for the halting of their monthly periods, they were clueless that they had missed the full effects of this rite of passage. Thus, they seemed oblivious and unsympathetic to the struggles I faced.

They say a woman's experience of menopause often follows what her own mother went through during this phase of her life. But in my case, my mother and even my elder sister had no recollection of what it was like to go through this season of life. With no reference points in my genealogy, it felt like I was talking to a brick wall. I felt utterly alone in this unfamiliar territory, desperately seeking support and understanding.

I found Dr. Mindy Pelz's book *The Menopause Reset* to be a valuable and personalized resource for managing menopause symptoms and improving overall health during this stage of life. However, I did find that implementing the information from the book was challenging without a strong sense of accountability. To supplement my reading, I joined several Facebook communities focused on menopause and even hosted a live segment on my own Facebook page featuring a retired nurse who affectionately refers to herself as the "Menopause Whisperer." During the thirty-minute episode, she shared practical tips and lifestyle changes that women can incorporate to alleviate menopause symptoms and rediscover joy in their lives. The episode received a significant number of views and generated numerous comments, highlighting the need for more open and honest conversations about menopause, particularly within the Black community.

As I journeyed through menopause, I encountered numerous challenging symptoms that made dating a nightmare. One of the most difficult was brain fog, which left me feeling less sharp and witty in conversations. I would often struggle to find the right words to complete my sentences, making me feel frustrated and self-conscious. Another major hurdle was the disruption to my sleep. I constantly had to adjust the air conditioning and fan throughout the night to find relief from the heat of my hot flashes. While I did experience occasional night sweats, they were not as intense as the daytime hot flashes. Finding a balance between feeling fresh and dealing with the hormonal changes my body was going through proved to be a constant struggle. On top of it all, I battled weight gain, particularly around my belly, breasts, back, and buttocks, despite my efforts to exercise and make lifestyle changes. It was a frustrating struggle that seemed to defy logic.

For three long years, I made several trips to my gynecologist, who recommended hormone replacement therapy (HRT) in several forms (pills, topical gel, and patches), but I decided against it. Although most research showed that short-term use of HRT was safe for relieving menopause symptoms, I remained firm in my decision not to use it.

I tried my best to push through these symptoms without resorting to prescription medication. I was hesitant to introduce any human-made hormones into my body since it was evident that my body was already turning on itself. Instead, I tried to school myself in better understanding what was best for me. I explored natural remedies: I drank herbal teas (such as black cohosh), increased my physical activity and water consumption, tried to get more sleep, and worked to manage my stress. I opted for loose clothing and cotton underwear to ensure breathability. I invested in cooling cloths that I kept in the refrigerator so I could ice my neck when a hot flash came on. While these methods provided some relief in the moment, they were not enough to alleviate all of my symptoms, which seemed to be getting stronger over time.

Eventually, I reached my breaking point. I was exhausted, both physically and mentally, from the constant discomfort and inconvenience. It had become unbearable to live like this with no end in sight. I was utterly miserable. I was sick and tired of being sick and tired. The constant perspiration had taken over my life, leaving me drenched in sweat even when I was simply standing still. The frustration of getting dressed, only to have my clothes soaked through before I even left the house, was overwhelming. Zoom calls became a source of anxiety as I would break out in a sweat, desperately trying to keep my face dry while leading a meeting. The simple act of wearing makeup or even a touch of powder seemed futile, as it would be instantly washed away, leaving no trace of the carefully applied cosmetics. The excessive sweating had also taken a toll on my skin, leaving it dry and thin, making it impossible to shave or even use a gentle loofah without causing bruises. I was beyond tired.

I found myself back in my gynecologist's office, desperate for relief. We revisited the options we had previously discussed, and I asked her to recap them for me. After careful consideration, I made the decision to try a compounded topical gel formula. This involved the formulation of a customized hormonal medication based on my specific hormone levels as determined by my blood work. Although I was initially hesitant, I knew I needed to find a solution that would alleviate my maddening symptoms. My doctor recommended an Arizona-based compounding pharmacy, Women's International Pharmacy, to fill the prescription. Compounding pharmacies create customized medications for individual patients by combining ingredients and adjusting dosage. They work closely with health care providers to develop medications that are not commercially available or to modify existing medications to meet specific patient needs. They offer personalized treatment options for patients with unique medication requirements.

Now that I am a few months into this regimen, I can confidently say that starting HRT has been a game changer for me. The difference it has made in my life is truly remarkable, like night and day. I went from experiencing about ten intense hot flashes a day to just a few mild ones that are easily manageable with my trusty handheld mini-fan. I finally feel like myself again, a feeling I didn't even realize I had lost.

Looking back, I can't help but reflect on the hesitation I had about starting HRT. I put myself through unnecessary suffering, thinking I could tough it out on my own. But now I realize that there was no need for me to endure all of that discomfort and frustration. Starting HRT has restored a sense of normalcy to my life that I didn't think was possible.

This experience has also made me more empathetic toward other women who are going through their own menopause journey. I now understand firsthand the challenges and struggles that come with this frequently misunderstood stage of life. It has given me a newfound appreciation for the importance of support and understanding during this time. I am grateful for the opportunity to share my story and offer comfort and empathy to women who may be going through similar experiences, especially those of us who are courageous enough to enter the dating arena.

Points to Ponder

- You are not alone! Menopause is a unique and personal journey all women must go through. Luckily, for some, it is literally a silent passage, while for others it is a blazing inferno. Dating during this stage of life can be challenging.

- Remember that menopause is a natural part of a woman's life cycle and that it is essential to embrace it rather than fight against it. Practice self-care and prioritize your well-being, seek out opportunities to learn and educate yourself on the issue, and share your knowledge with others. This will help you navigate this phase of your life with grace and understanding.

Epilogue

I can do all this through him who gives me strength.

PHILIPPIANS 4:13

As I reflect on the completion of this book, I can't help but feel a sense of accomplishment and gratitude. It has been a transformative journey, not just for me as the author but also for the countless women who will read these pages and find solace during their own seasons of waiting.

Throughout the process, I have come to understand the power of vulnerability and the impact that sharing our stories can have on others. It takes courage to bare your soul to the world, to expose your fears and insecurities, but it is in that vulnerability that true connection and healing can take place.

While my own love story has yet to unfold, I have learned that waiting does not mean inaction. In fact, it is a time for growth, self-discovery, and preparation. I have embraced this season of singleness as an opportunity to practice self-love and gratitude daily and to inspire other women who are walking a similar path to do the same.

I want every reader to know that she is not alone in her journey. There is a sisterhood of women who understand the highs and lows, the hopes and doubts that come with waiting for love. Together, we can support and encourage one another as we navigate this often challenging road.

May this book serve as a reminder that you are deserving of a love that surpasses all expectations. Embrace your season of waiting, knowing that it is leading you closer to the fulfillment of God's promise for your life. Keep the faith, stay patient, and never forget that your love story is unfolding exactly as it should.

As you close this book, I encourage you to take the inspiration you have found within these pages and turn it into action. Take those small, actionable steps toward the life you desire. Believe wholeheartedly that love, in its perfect timing, will find its way to you.

Remember that your value as a woman is not defined by your relationship status. You are whole and complete on your own. Trust in the process, have faith in the journey, and hold onto the belief that the love you desire is worth every moment of the W.A.I.T.

My Prayer

> This is the confidence we have in approaching God: that if we ask anything according to his will, he hears us. And if we know that He hears us—whatever we ask—we know that we have what we asked of him.
>
> 1 JOHN 5:14–15

Dear Heavenly Father,

It's me. I stand before you right now with a heart full of hope in you and a deep desire to find a loving and godly husband. I know that you have a perfect plan for my life and that this, like every season in my life, is purposely designed by you.

Lord, I surrender the spirit of anxiousness, fear, doubt, and longing for a husband into your hands as I know that you are the greatest matchmaker and that you have someone special prepared for me. Bless me with a patient and content sprit in this season of waiting as you work behind the scenes to bring us together.

I pray that the words you have placed within the pages

of this book become a testimony for other women on their journey of singleness. May this book serve as a source of encouragement and inspiration for these women.

Father, please help to prepare me to be a loving and supportive wife. Shower me with wisdom, kindness, and grace so that I may be a blessing to my future husband.

Lord, help me to guard my heart and to always seek your guidance and discernment as I navigate the world of dating. Let me never entertain the desire to take matters into my own hands, settle for less, or take the easy way out. Help me to easily spot the qualities of a godly man and the courage to promptly run away from those who are not aligned with my core values and from those who attempt to erode my boundaries.

Father, I pray for my future husband right now. Please bless him, protect him, and draw him closer to you each day. Prepare his heart to be a loving and faithful husband and help him to grow in his relationship with you. Surround him with godly influences and grant him wisdom in his own search for a life partner.

Lord, your timing is always perfect as your will is being done. Please allow me to be joyful, hopeful, and faithful in my journey of singleness as each step brings me closer to you and the fulfillment of my heart's desire.

In Jesus' name, I pray. Amen.

Resources for Further Exploration

Over the years, I have tapped into the resources below as well as many others as guides and inspiration along my single journey.

BOOKS

In addition to a vast array of versions of the Holy Bible, I have also consulted the following books.

Batterson, Mark. *Draw the Circle: The 40 Day Prayer Challenge.* Grand Rapids, MI: Zondervan, 2015.

Chapman, Gary. *The 5 Love Languages: The Secret to Love That Lasts.* Woodmere, NY: Northfield Publishing, 2015.

Chole, Alicia Britt. *The Night Is Normal: A Guide through Spiritual Pain.* Carol Stream, IL: Tyndale Refresh, 2023.

Harvey, Steve. *Act Like a Lady, Think Like a Man: What Men Really Think About Love, Relationships, Intimacy, and Commitment.* New York: HarperCollins, 2014.

Pelz, Mindy. *The Menopause Reset: Get Rid of Your Symptoms and Feel Like Your Younger Self Again.* Carlsbad, CA: Hay House, 2023.

Shirer, Priscilla. *Fervent: A Woman's Battle Plan to Serious, Specific and Strategic Prayer.* Nashville, TN: B&H Publishing Group, 2015.

Spellen, T. C. *The Waiting Room: A 31-Day Devotional for Single Women Waiting for the Right Husband.* Brooklyn, NY: TCS Publishing, 2012.

PEOPLE AND ORGANIZATIONS I FOLLOW

Cindy Trimm Ministries
https://cindytrimmministries.org
"As a global organization, Cindy Trimm Ministries International is dedicated to the service of humanity. The primary goal is to expand the kingdom of God."

Love Life with Matthew Hussey
https://matthewhussey.com
"Love Life with Matthew Hussey" is a weekly podcast that "shares practical advice, hard-won wisdom, and the occasional musing on relationships and the increasingly confusing world of modern dating." Hussey also has a membership program for women; it is also called Love Life.

Mindvalley
https://www.mindvalley.com
"Mindvalley is the world's most powerful life transformation platform. It features a global community of changemakers who support you."

Motivating the Masses
https://motivatingthemasses.com
"Founder Lisa Nichols is committed to having you do the things you have never done before so you can get the results you have never had and create the life you only dream of."

Stephan Speaks
https://www.stephanspeaks.com
"Stephan Labossiere's mission is to make relationships happier and more fulfilling."

About the Author

Vanessa Ingrid Farrell is a speaker, best-selling author, and CEO and founder of Vanessa Ingrid (VI) Health & Wellness Coaching, LLC. Her coaching practice helps busy women, especially those in leadership roles, unapologetically prioritize and preserve their heart health without sacrificing career and the joys of everyday life experiences.

Vanessa loves journaling and is a trained journal coach. She has created and published many journals. She has been journaling for over thirty years and is a member of the International Association for Journal Writing. She facilitates individual, and group journaling sessions and workshops.

Vanessa was born on the beautiful island of Montserrat in the Caribbean and currently resides on the island of St. Croix in the United States Virgin Islands.

Vanessa is available virtually and in person for speaking engagements, workshops, and retreats.

You can reach Vanessa at VFarrell@VIHealthcoaching.com.

Visit her website and online journal store at www.vihealthcoaching.com.

www.ingramcontent.com/pod-product-compliance
Lightning Source LLC
Chambersburg PA
CBHW071211160426
43196CB00011B/2262